The Story *of* Redemption

VOLUME 1 • GENESIS - 2 SAMUEL

KRISTIN SCHMUCKER & MIRANDA MAE EWING

From Genesis to Revelation, the Bible tells us the story of redemption. It reminds us of who we are and teaches us of the God who has pursued us from the beginning of time. Despite all the times we have failed, He has remained faithful. In the first pages of Genesis, we see God's good creation, the devastation of the fall, and the promise of the Redeemer who would come and make everything right. His name is Jesus—and He changes everything. We learn about Him throughout the entire Old Testament. Then in the New Testament, He bursts onto the scene, and we are overwhelmed with who He is. The Bible is the story of our redemption. But more importantly, the Bible is the story of the God of redemption.

The Story of Redemption is a Bible reading companion that walks through the entire Bible, chapter by chapter. It is for anyone who has ever wanted to read the entire Bible and for everyone who has started to read through the Bible but felt overwhelmed. It is also for anyone who wants to understand the full story of Scripture and see Jesus on every page.

It is our prayer that as you read Scripture, you will see it as one cohesive story that all points to our Redeemer. Jesus is the center of Scripture, and we see Him revealed to us on every page of the Bible. He is the one who every saint in the Old Testament anticipated. He is the one who came into the world to pay for our redemption in the New Testament. And now He is the one we place our faith in as we await the day when He will make all things right—and we will worship Him face to face for all of eternity. He has kept every promise. He has done all that He has said He would do. He has never changed. He has pursued us in steadfast love. He has been faithful.

This story is *unlike any other story.*

This is the *story of Jesus.*

This is the *story of redemption.*

Contents

God
planned
it for good.

Genesis

GENRE: Law, Historical Narrative

AUTHOR / DATE WRITTEN

Moses • c. 1440-1400 BC

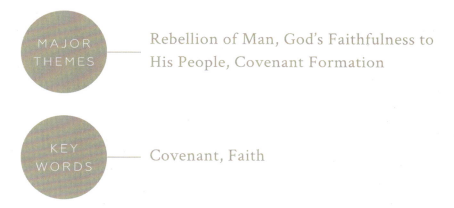

MAJOR THEMES — Rebellion of Man, God's Faithfulness to His People, Covenant Formation

KEY WORDS — Covenant, Faith

KEY VERSE

GENESIS 50:20

You planned evil against me; God planned it for
good to bring about the present result — the survival
of many people.

Genesis 1-3

The very first verse on the very first page starts with God. Creation declares that the gospel is all about God. The New Testament shows us that these first words speak of Jesus as the Creator (John 1:1-3, Colossians 1:15-17). From the start, we learn God is the God of order as He systematically speaks the world into existence. Man and woman are created in the image of God, the *imago Dei*, and are made distinct from the rest of creation (Genesis 1:26). After creation, God rests, which serves to shift the focus from the creation to the glory of the Creator.

The scene changes in chapter 3 with the fall of man. Here we are introduced to a sneaky serpent who will deceive Eve. The forbidden fruit is eaten by Eve and then by Adam—and everything changes. But in Genesis 3:15, a promise is given that will change everything. It is a promise of redemption and a redeemer. This verse is the protoevangelium, which means that it is the first mention of the gospel. All of creation now waits for the Promised One. The Messiah will come someday and right every wrong. Genesis 3:21 points to the truth found in Hebrews 9:22 and illustrates the need for redemption that would later come through Jesus Christ. When Adam and Eve disobey God, they find themselves ashamed of their nakedness. The Lord clothes them with the skin of a slaughtered animal, demonstrating the horrific reality of sin and the penalty for breaking His law. A payment or atonement is required, and here we see the grace of God in providing a substitute in an animal. It is the first substitution and a reminder that we could never atone for our sin, but God in His mercy has provided a way for our sin to be covered. The image of a slain animal points us forward to the Lamb of God, who will cover the sins of God's people. It is the first substitution and a reminder that we could never atone for our sin, but God in His mercy has provided a way for our sin to be covered. The image of a slain animal points us forward to the Lamb of God, who will cover the sins of God's people.

In these first three chapters of the Bible, everything rapidly changes. Adam and Eve must leave the garden, but it is not without the promise that someday Jesus will come and make everything right. The first Adam serves to point our hearts to the second and better Adam (1 Corinthians 15:22-23, Romans 5:12-21). The story that is about to unfold points us to Jesus. The story is one of God coming to rescue and redeem His people. The story of redemption begins with the promise of the Redeemer.

"The story that is about to unfold points us to Jesus."

Think for a moment on what a privilege it is to be made in the image of God (Genesis 1:26). How can this fact change your perception regarding why personal sanctification is important?

2. Genesis 2:15 describes God placing man in the garden of Eden to work it and watch over it. Notice this happened before the fall; work is not a result of sin. How does this change your perception of earthly work? How does this shape your view of what heaven will be like?

3. The serpent convinced Adam and Eve that his word was truer than what God had said. What voices do you allow to speak with too much authority in your life?

Genesis 4-6

As we continue the book of Genesis, the world is declining. Things are getting worse, and things are getting worse fast.

We are introduced to Cain and Abel, the sons of Adam and Eve. The brothers bring sacrifices, and Abel's is accepted while Cain's is not. We do not know exactly why Cain's sacrifice is not accepted, but we know from Hebrews 11:4 that Abel came in faith. God accepted Abel's offering. Cain kills his brother, Abel, and as a result of the murder, Cain is cursed. Just one chapter after the fall, we see that murder has already taken place. This serves to point us to humanity's desperate need for God. And despite our sin, God would still make a way for the Messiah to come. As part of that redemption story, God gives Adam and Eve another son named Seth.

Chapter 5 shows us a genealogy with a long list of names. Though it is tempting to skip these Scripture passages, this genealogy marks an essential truth for us about life after the fall. Because of what sin had done, people now live and die, just as God said. The consequence of sin is always death, and the genealogy demonstrates that. Yet, tucked in the genealogy is a man named Enoch who walked with God and then was gone. It is mysterious, and yet it points to the truth that God is stronger than this pattern of sin and death.

It is through the lineage of Seth that Noah is born. Many generations had passed, and the world had continued to slip further and further into sin. The world had become more and more wicked, but one man "found favor in the eyes of the Lord." His name is Noah, and the favor that He found was God's grace. God tells Noah a flood is coming, and then He commands Noah to build an ark. It all seems a little crazy, but Noah did everything God commanded him to do. His life is a reminder to us to trust the Lord even when it does not make sense and rest in the grace that He has shown us.

"God is stronger than this pattern of sin and death."

While we do not know precisely why Cain's sacrifice was not accepted, can you think of ways that the sacrifices of your own heart may grieve the Lord in the same way?

Genesis 6:8 tells us that Noah found favor, or grace, in the eyes of the Lord. Where have you found grace with the Lord?

Dwell for a moment on the last verse of chapter 6. How can you learn from Noah's faithfulness and obedience to the task God commanded him to do?

Genesis 7-9

Noah is a great example of faith.

He had likely never even experienced rain, and yet he built a boat anticipating the rain that would fall from the sky as God had promised. He trusted in God even though he did not understand (Hebrews 11:7). Noah built the ark, and the rain came. The ark is a beautiful picture of the safety and security of salvation in Jesus, and its one door reminds us of the one way to salvation.

Noah and his family were not exempt from the floodwaters, but God brought them through in the safety and security of the ark (1 Peter 3:20). After the flood, Noah built an altar to the Lord, and God made a covenant never to destroy the earth by flood again. Then, God set a rainbow in the sky as a reminder of the covenant He had made. It is a reminder to us of His faithfulness, but it is also a reminder to Himself of His promise (Genesis 9:16). We can be confident that He is always faithful to His children. Even when we fail—as Noah did at the end of chapter 9—God's favor and faithfulness is based on who God is and not on what we do. He is always faithful.

Noah's story points us to Jesus. Just like Noah, Jesus obeyed the will of God and created a way to rescue all who believe His message. The ark is a picture of salvation. The wood of this boat points us to the wood of the cross. There, Jesus bears the weight of the punishment that we deserved just as the ark bears the downpours of rain. As believers, we rest safe and secure inside the salvation that Jesus brings. Though the floods come, we can rest safely in Him. Noah and his family were not exceptionally good people, and we are reminded of that as we see Noah's sin. Noah was not a perfect man, but he was a man who God showered in grace, and he was a man who placed his faith in the promise of deliverance. What a beautiful picture for us who have placed our faith in God's overflowing and undeserved grace.

"Noah's story points us to Jesus."

Though Noah likely had never experienced rain, he followed God's command to build a boat in faithfulness. How can this encourage you in your faithfulness with your walk with God?

In Genesis 8:21, the Lord proclaims His promise to never again curse the ground because of human beings, citing that man is evil from youth onward. Take a moment to think about the condition of your own heart — where it was before salvation and where was it afterward. If you have never trusted Jesus to be your Savior, consider whether this is the time to do so. How does this passage expand your understanding of God's grace to us?

In chapter 9, we learn that the rainbow is God's reminder of His promise and covenant. What are some symbolic reminders God has given you that aid you in remembering His faithfulness to keep His promises?

Genesis 10-12

Several generations pass, and we come to the Tower of Babel, where everyone alive on earth was gathered in one location.

In Genesis 11:4, we learn they desired to build a tower to reach the heavens. At first glance, it may seem like the plan is not bad, but it was direct disobedience to the command to fill the earth (Genesis 1:28). They wanted to stay where they were and make a great name for themselves, but God had another plan. God would confuse their languages and disperse them throughout the earth. The people wanted to make a name for themselves, but God wanted them to glorify His name.

The first eleven chapters of the book of Genesis show the problem of sin getting worse and worse, but the start of chapter 12 includes a significant shift. We are introduced to Abram, who is one of the most important characters in Scripture. The Lord commanded Abram to leave his country and everything that he knew to go to the place that God would show him. God promises Abram that He would make his name great and bless all the families of the earth through him. These first verses of Genesis 12 are known as the Abrahamic covenant, and we should etch these verses in our minds as we continue through Scripture and see the fulfillment of this covenant. This covenant with Abram was unconditional. It was not dependent on what Abram would do but on who God is. The theme of redemption is starting to build, and that veiled promise given in Genesis 3:15 of the One who would crush the head of the serpent is beginning to become just a bit clearer. All families of the earth would be blessed through Abram because it was through him that the Messiah would come. Jesus comes and changes everything (Galatians 3:8, 14, Psalm 72:17). Abram is a great example to us of faith (Hebrews 11:8-12). Abram followed the Lord even though he did not know where he was going or how all of God's promises would come about. He is a reminder to us to trust the Lord no matter what.

"Jesus comes and changes everything."

In chapter 10, we read another genealogy. This reminds us that Noah's faith-filled obedience left behind a legacy to his family. How will your family remember your obedience to the Lord? Does your life testify that God's will is supreme?

Genesis 12:1-3 are some of the most important verses in Scripture. How is this promise fulfilled in Jesus?

When we sin, its effect does not remain contained to our own lives. What does Genesis 12:10-20 tell us about how our sin—in this case, lying—can have a snowball effect on the lives around us?

Genesis 13-15

God will fulfill every single promise that He makes, but it will not always be in the way that Abram anticipates. In chapters 13 and 14, we are given glimpses into the life of Abraham and Lot and introduced to Melchizedek. In chapter 15, God comes to Abram in a vision, reminding him of the promises that will be fulfilled. Abram is confused. He does not understand how he will have an heir when he and his wife are aging and still childless. He wonders if it will be his servant, but God reassures him that it will be his own son. This is a confusing situation for Abram. God promised Abram that his descendants would be like the stars in the sky, yet Abram and his wife did not have a child and were quite advanced in age. And people who are nearly a hundred years old do not generally have children. How could God's promises be fulfilled?

In an act of faith, Abram believes the Lord (Genesis 15:6, Romans 4:18-22). Scripture tells us that his faith was counted to him as righteousness. This does not mean that he was made righteous by his faith, but God imputed, or credited, righteousness to him because of his faith. In the same way, Jesus imputes His righteousness to us when we trust in Him for our salvation (2 Corinthians 5:21). Abram serves as an example of justification by faith. As chapter 15 closes, we see a covenant ceremony take place, but the interesting thing to note is that during this important ceremony, Abram is asleep. It serves as a beautiful picture and reminder to us that this covenant was dependent solely on God.

Abram believed in the Messiah who would come, and we can believe in the Messiah who has come. From the beginning of Genesis, God set a plan in place, and the One who would deliver us was promised. And just as it was true in Abram's day, the promises of God are dependent not on what we do but on who He is.

"Abram believed in the Messiah who would come, and we can believe in the Messiah who has come."

In Genesis 13:2, we learn that Abram was a rich man, and in 13:4b, we learn that Abram called upon the name of the Lord. Reflect upon your earthly possessions. Do you find your delight in God like Abram? Or, do any of these things distract you from calling on the name of the Lord?

Genesis 14:22 shows Abram keeping an oath he made to the Lord. How can we learn from Abram's faithfulness here? Do you find it easy or challenging to keep your promises, whether to God or man?

In Genesis 15, we see that God promises to be faithful to His covenant and that the covenant is fully dependent on God and not on Abram (Abraham). How does this give you confidence that God will be faithful to you?

Genesis 16-18

God made a promise that, from the perspective of man, seemed impossible.

However, with the Lord, nothing is impossible. Abram and Sarai were old, and with each passing month, the possibility of having a son seemed to diminish. Abram must have been so confused, and Sarai must have felt responsible for this dream that was not coming to fruition. Sarai concocted a plan that she thought would accomplish what she could not do on her own. But she failed to realize that she never had to do it on her own. In His power, God would accomplish the promise that He had made.

Our plans and schemes will never give joy the way that God's plans will. In these chapters, we are reminded again of the covenant that God made to Abram. Even though Abram and Sarai tried to do things their way, in their strength, and not according to God's plan, Abram and Sarai's names were changed to Abraham and Sarah as God again assured them that He always keeps His promises. It may not be in the timing we expect. It may not be in the way we expect. But He will do what He has promised.

These chapters, over and over again, point us to the God of covenant. He is the one who sees the outcast and the broken. Just as He met Hagar at the well, He is the one who gives and keeps covenant, and throughout chapter 17, we see God speaking of everything He would do. Over and over, we see the personal pronoun "I," followed by a description of what God would do. The covenant promises were never dependent on Abram and Sarai but on the Lord. Later in chapter 17, we see the promise of a miraculous birth that would point to an even more miraculous birth in the future. In Genesis 18:14, we see almost the exact words spoken by Mary in Luke 1:37 as a reminder directly from the Lord that He is powerful and will fulfill His promises. And in that very same verse is a reminder that God would bring His promises about at the appointed time. Nearly the same language is used throughout the New Testament for how Jesus came at the appointed time (Romans 5:6). God always comes through at just the right time.

In Genesis 16:13, we see the name of God as "the one who sees me." Do you find comfort or discomfort in the fact that our lives are transparent before God? Does your reaction to this spur you on toward holiness and sanctification?

God made a weighty and seemingly impossible promise to Abraham, and Abraham scoffed at Him while God remained honest to His word. In what ways are you fighting against trusting God's promises in your life in this season? Does God's faithfulness to fulfill His promises to Abraham encourage you to trust God more?

At the end of chapter 18, we are reminded that God delights in the righteousness of His people. When asked if God would spare an entire evil city on account of ten righteous people, the Lord confirms that He would. What does this tell us about God's desires for righteousness?

Genesis 19-21

Today's passage starts with the story of Lot. It is a heavy story, but we are reminded of God's faithfulness in caring for and protecting His people and the seriousness of sin.

After the opening, the story then shifts back to Abraham, and we see the long-awaited promise of a son fulfilled. John 8:56 tells us that Abraham saw Jesus's day, and truly Abraham saw with the eyes of faith the promise fulfilled through the miraculous birth of the promised son, Isaac. The birth of Isaac was a miracle that could come only from God. It is a glimpse of what would later come in Jesus. The miraculous birth of Isaac pointed to a far greater miracle that would take place at the virgin birth. The Jewish people would be able to look back to Isaac and the promise that was kept to Abraham and trust that God would also keep His promises to them and send the Messiah, the Promised One.

In chapter 21, we also see God's provision to Hagar and Ishmael in the wilderness. In her impatience and sin, Sarah brought about a terrible situation by coercing Abraham to follow her plan instead of trusting in God's sovereign plan. But God would not abandon Hagar and Ishmael. The God who sees would see them and protect them.

God always keeps His promises. This is the message we learn from the life of Abraham. Back in Genesis 12 and 15, we saw a great covenant made with Abraham. Here in chapter 21, we are again reminded of an offspring who would come from Isaac. Galatians 3:16 tells us plainly that this offspring is Jesus. He is the one who God promised to Abraham so long ago. Now, we can also look back and see the lives of Isaac and Jesus and know that God always keeps His promises. He does what He says He will do. He will not fail us. He will never let us down. And though it may not always happen in the way or in the timing that we expect—He will be faithful. We do not have to take matters into our own hands. We do not have to worry that the path ahead seems impossible. We must trust Him. We can be faithful right where we are and know that He will be faithful to every word of His promises. The covenant-keeping God will not let us down.

"God always keeps His promises."

In chapter 19, we see God spare Lot. What does this tell us about God's character?

Genesis 20:12 describes Abraham's attempt to justify his lie about Sarah being his sister based on a technicality. Meditate on ways that you might also do that with God. Do you live as though God sees your every moment?

In chapter 21, we see that God has fulfilled His promise to Abraham as he fathered a child borne of Sarah. This was a long-awaited gift, but God was nevertheless faithful. How does your understanding of God's timing practically apply to what you may be waiting on in different seasons of your life?

Genesis 22-24

Genesis 22 opens with God asking Abraham to do what seems impossible.

The Lord asks Abraham to offer Isaac as a sacrifice. Can you imagine the turmoil taking place in Abraham's heart and mind? God had promised to make a great nation of him. He had promised that a Messiah would come through his line. But Abraham only had one son. He had one miracle child, and now he was being asked to sacrifice Isaac. Yet, he obeyed. Perhaps it was because he had seen time and time again the Lord prove His faithfulness. So, he did what the Lord asked and began the journey. Abraham built the altar and bound Isaac, but as he raised the knife, a voice from heaven stopped him. Abraham's words proved to be true — God would provide a lamb. And, it is here that Abraham sees a ram caught in the thicket.

In the same way that God provided that ram, He one day provides Jesus, the perfect Lamb of God. This event shows the powerful truth of the Lamb as our substitution. Jesus would be the perfect Lamb of God, the once for all sacrifice (Hebrews 10:12). Abraham trusted that God would make a way. Just as in the past, he did not know how it would happen, but he knew that God would fulfill His promises (Hebrews 11:17-19). Genesis 22 is a story, not about Abraham's great faith or what Abraham did for God but a story about what God did for Abraham and ultimately, what God accomplishes for His people on the cross with the sacrifice of His own beloved Son.

God provides for His people. He is faithful to His covenant promises. God continues to provide for Isaac, and chapter 24 shows the Lord providing a wife, Rebekah. Time and time again, we see that God is faithful. He will never fail the people He has called. The Messiah comes through the line of Isaac, and God was faithful every step of the way to sovereignly guide every piece of the grand story of redemption.

"God provides for His people. He is faithful to His covenant promises."

QUESTIONS

Meditate on this: "God himself will provide the lamb for the burnt offering, my son" (Genesis 22:8a). Abraham bet his son's life on God's promises. Reflect on what it means to truly obey God amid confusion.

In chapter 23, we see that Sarah dies, and we see Abraham purchase a small plot of land where he can bury her. This burial plot is located in the Promised Land from Genesis 12:7. How does this act speak to God's sovereignty in designating a burial plot in the land promised for the patriarchs?

In chapter 25, we once again see the Lord's provision for Abraham, this time through finding his son a wife. We see how clear God made it to his servant that Rebekah was the woman set aside for Isaac. Think for a moment on the interruption the servant caused in Rebekah's life, and then contemplate how willing she was to go where God called her to go. How does this expand your understanding of obedience to God and His conviction for your life?

Genesis 25-27

In chapter 25, we are introduced to Jacob.

Isaac prayed to the Lord when Rebekah was barren, and then Rebekah conceived twins. God was making it clear that the fulfillment of His covenant would be His work. Even during Rebekah's pregnancy, the brothers struggle with each other in the womb. The Lord promised something out of the ordinary when He says that the older will serve the younger. This family definitely had its fair share of dysfunction as Isaac favors Esau, and Rebekah favors Jacob. As the tension grows, Esau sells his birthright for a bowl of stew. Near the end of Isaac's life, when he is almost blind, the time comes for a son to be blessed. God had promised a special blessing for Jacob, but it seems that Isaac did not want to follow God's plan. In the meantime, Rebekah made a plot of her own to ensure Jacob would be the one to receive the blessing.

All of the members in the family had their own sin and plan. But in the end, it was the Lord's plan that prevailed. Even though we are not always faithful, the Lord is always faithful. He always does what He says He will do. Despite the sin that prevailed in this family—from Rebekah's desire to control to favoritism to disunity—God is faithful to His covenant promises. God set His love on Jacob despite his sin and manipulation. What a reminder of God's grace to us as His people. He sets His love and favor on us despite our sin, and He chose us to be His before we were even born.

Again, the Bible reminds us that the promises of God are not dependent on us. God's promises are solely and fully dependent on Him. We neither need to manipulate to receive His promises nor try to run from them. He is faithful to His promises. Despite the unlikely family tree, God uses this misfit family of Abraham to bring the Messiah. Jesus, the King of kings, would come just as God had promised—to bring hope and restoration. Blessing through Jesus comes through this unlikely family, showing God's sovereignty.

"Again, the Bible reminds us that the promises of God are not dependent on us."

24

Reflect on the faithfulness of God versus the faithfulness of man. How does God's faithfulness spur you on toward conforming your ways to His likeness?

Think about the amount of time that passed between God's first covenant to Abraham and His reaffirmation of this covenant to Isaac. What can you learn about God's character from this?

In chapter 27, we learn a lot about man's propensity for deceitfulness. How does seeing this play out teach you about God's faithfulness to His covenant despite our sinfulness?

Genesis 28-30

Jacob's life was full of struggle, and though He was raised in a family who knew the Lord, it was not until he had a dream that he truly met the Lord for himself.

When God met Jacob in that dream, Jacob encountered his God and not just the God of his father and grandfather. Jacob's dream also foreshadows the true gate of heaven (John 1:48-51). God promised Jacob that all families on the earth would be blessed through his offspring—and that promised offspring is Jesus. Jacob renamed the location of his dream Bethel, which means House of God, and the location would be important later in his story. God met Jacob in Bethel and confirmed the promises made to his grandfather. God had not forgotten His covenant and was still working His plan to bring the Redeemer.

The scene then shifts, and Jacob is looking for a wife. He promised to work seven years for Rachel but is tricked into marrying her sister, Leah. He is forced to work another seven years for Rachel. The story is bitter to read because no one wants to feel unwanted or rejected, but we cling to the promise that in Jesus, we are accepted. Rachel struggles to bear children, and Leah had many in hopes of gaining the favor of her husband. The birth of Judah changes something in her, and Leah gave him a name that means "this time I will praise the Lord." Somehow she must have known that for all the sorrow that she had faced, this son of hers would be the one through whom the Messiah, Jesus, would come. Truly, she had a reason to give praise.

Even when we do not understand, His ways are good. He can use even our sorrow to bring about our greatest joy. Leah and Rachel both felt rejection in different ways, and yet God saw both of them. The family tree of the Messiah would be built through these women. They are even mentioned together in Ruth 4:11 as having built the house of Israel. Their stories are stories of pain and stories of purpose and hope in a God who sees and is faithful to His promises.

"Even when we do not understand, His ways are good."

In Genesis 28:20, we see Jacob making a vow that if God provides for him, he will worship Him. Think back on your moment of salvation, and then remember the times God has been faithful to provide for you. Did you make a vow to worship only Him? If so, have you kept your vow to worship only Him because He has been faithful to you?

Think about the name, Judah, meaning "This time I will praise the Lord." Reflect on the resignation to God's will that Leah had during this time. How can you praise God amid struggle?

Many of us can probably relate to Rachel or Leah. Each in her circumstances felt overlooked, forgotten, or unlucky. Though their worth was fluid in the eyes of the world, we see that God continually tended to what they needed. In what ways have you experienced God tending to your specific needs when you are feeling sorrow?

Genesis 31-33

Through the life of Jacob, we repeatedly see struggle.

However, Jacob's life is a reminder that living a life of blessing does not mean living a life free of sorrow or struggle. Though Jacob was clearly chosen to receive a special blessing from God, he also experienced intense struggle. Some of it was brought about due to his actions, and some of it was by no fault of his own. Jacob fled from Laban and the injustice he was experiencing there and followed God's leading. It is interesting to note that as God speaks to Jacob in a dream, He reminds Jacob of what had happened at Bethel. The God who had been faithful to Jacob in the past was gently assuring him of His faithfulness in the present and His faithfulness to come.

Jacob headed back to the land of his birth to see his brother, Esau. He did not know what would happen when he encountered the brother he had cheated. But before he encounters Esau, he meets someone else on his journey.

We come to an odd account of Jacob wrestling with God. This was a pre-incarnate appearance of Jesus, which means that it is Jesus before He came to earth in the New Testament. Jacob wrestles with the Lord all night long and pleads for a blessing from the One who he was wrestling. The Lord did bless him. However, He also left Jacob with a permanent reminder of the night he struggled with the Lord. Jacob was willing to do whatever it took to receive the blessing of God. Yes, Jacob's life was full of struggle and hardship, but it also overflowed with the blessing and favor of His God. He could always look back to the night when he met his God face to face.

Jacob's life of struggle is one part of the story that would culminate in the Messiah, and though Jacob was far from perfect, God showered him in grace and brought the Messiah through his line. Not only that, but Jesus uniquely appeared to Jacob. God had not forgotten His promise to Abraham, Isaac, and Jacob. Every moment of the journey was worked together by God.

"Every moment of the journey was worked together by God."

QUESTIONS

Jacob and Laban's covenant seems to be different from the covenants that we have seen God make with man. Take a moment to compare and contrast the ways that this covenant is both similar and different to God's covenants with man.

What can we learn about God from Jacob's persistence in wrestling until he was blessed? What can we learn about the importance of persisting in our personal "wrestling" with God?

In chapter 33, we see the reunion of Esau and Jacob. What can we learn from Esau about joy-filled forgiveness? How can we apply that to those who have wounded us?

Genesis 34-36

Our passage begins with the tragic account of Dinah. Our hearts ache for the brokenness caused by sin and this young woman who is assaulted.

The tragic account reminds us that our God is the only one who can bring true comfort to the hurting and the oppressed. Dinah's father and brothers failed to protect her or ease her suffering in any meaningful way. However, we have hope in our suffering. Jesus is the one who has suffered in our place to give us peace with God. Not only does He know what it means to suffer, but He has suffered on earth.

Tucked between the tragedy of Dinah and the deaths of Rachel and Isaac, there is a ray of hope and a reminder of God's faithfulness even through the hardships of life. The Lord blessed Jacob and gave him a new name. In Genesis 28:15, the Lord promises to be with Jacob and bless all the earth's families through him. Now, in Genesis 35:3, Jacob proclaims that God had been with him every step of the way. God always keeps His promises. He is always faithful—even when we are not.

Jacob made an altar to the Lord at Bethel, and then the Lord gave him a new name. He came back to the place of God's faithfulness and saw God's faithfulness to him again. He would no longer be called Jacob; he would now be called Israel. The Lord would also renew the covenant that He had made with Jacob. Even though Jacob faced struggle and hardship, he had also found that God is always faithful. The same is true for us. This life may not be easy, but we can trust the Lord. We can be confident in the plan that He has and know that He will do good— because He is good.

God was at work. Even when sin and tragedy seem to overwhelm the storyline, God was working behind the scenes to bring about His covenant promises. The promise of a child to come through Abraham had seemed impossible, yet now, chapters later, we are seeing the building of a family line. This family was not perfect, but through them would come the perfect One. This family was broken and fractured by sin, but the One was coming who would heal brokenness and break the power of sin.

"The One was coming who would heal brokenness and break the power of sin."

Chapter 34 is heavy and sorrowful. Thankfully, the story does not end there—redemption is coming. In light of the whole of Scripture, what does this chapter teach us about navigating through extreme circumstances of suffering?

In renewing His covenant with Jacob, God changes his name to Israel. Reflect on how Israel's very name was a constant reminder of God's faithfulness to His people.

Chapter 36 is largely another genealogy. Take another moment to reflect on these names. Though we do not know their whole story, they were used by God in Scripture. How can this comfort you in your daily, mundane work?

Genesis 37-39

Joseph's life points us to Jesus. We will see him suffer yet remain confident that God is always with him. In chapter 37, we meet Joseph as the favored son at only seventeen years old. He has a dream that his brothers and family would one day bow down to him. This infuriates his already jealous brothers. The brothers plan to kill him but end up throwing him into a pit and selling him into slavery.

The story briefly pauses as chapter 38 tells us the account of Jacob's son, Judah, and his daughter-in-law, Tamar. In a tragic and unlikely series of events, the mourning Tamar is mistaken for a prostitute by her father-in-law, who did not recognize her, and she becomes pregnant by him. But the quick-thinking Tamar held hostage a few of Judah's items that protect her from the capital punishment Judah had demanded before realizing that this was his own child; consequently, Judah realizes that Tamar is far more righteous than he. This account provides additional evidence that the brokenness of this family abounds. Yet, despite another tragedy, God is working. Tamar's name is found in Matthew 1 as part of the genealogy of Jesus. God uses broken people and messed up situations to bring about His sovereign plan.

Back in Egypt, Joseph's story continues. The Lord was with Joseph (Genesis 39:2). Joseph ends up in the home of Potiphar, who was an Egyptian and the captain of the guard. The Lord caused everything Joseph did to be successful. Even when Potiphar's wife tempts Joseph, he proves to be a man of integrity and does not sin against Potiphar or the Lord. As a result, Joseph is wrongfully put in prison, but again the Lord was with Him (Genesis 39:21). God is working through every moment.

Through all of Joseph's life, through all of Tamar's life, and yes, through all of our lives—God is with us. Even in hardship, or undeserved suffering, we can trust that the Lord will never leave us. He will never fail His own.

"He will never fail His own."

In chapter 37, we see that Joseph has a dream sent from God that foretells his adult life. Despite the suffering that Joseph endures, what can we learn about God's plans?

Reflect on the fact that Tamar is included in the genealogy of Jesus in Matthew 1. What does this tell you about how God works His plan through all circumstances?

After we read about Joseph's wrongful imprisonment, we are met with the verse, "But the Lord was with Joseph and extended kindness to him" (Genesis 39:21a). Reflect on some of the ways that God has extended kindness to you when you have experienced suffering. Spend some time in prayer, thanking Him for consoling you in your suffering.

Genesis 40-42

"God will work every part of our lives and every chapter of our stories for our good and His glory."

However, even in prison, Joseph finds favor with the Lord, and the Lord was with him (Genesis 39:21). The God in His sovereign providence would use every single part of Joseph's story for a purpose. Joseph's story is a constant reminder of how the Lord works, bringing people and events into the lives of his children at just the perfect moment. In prison, Joseph meets two men from the king's service, and he correctly interprets their dreams. The chief cupbearer to the king promises to remember Joseph, but when he is released, he forgets Joseph. Joseph waits in prison. Two years later, when the king has a dream, the cupbearer remembers his promise, and Joseph is called to interpret the dream. Joseph is then lifted to power and made second in command in the entire nation of Israel. This foreign king clearly sees that God was with Joseph.

When a famine strikes, Joseph's brothers come to Egypt. As they bow before Joseph, his heart must have been reminded of his dream and amazed at how the Lord had been with him every step of the way. This shows us that we can trust God even when we do not understand. He will be with us and keep His promises.

Just as Joseph would be the cherished son who would provide for the needs of His people though they had rejected him, so Jesus is the one rejected by men and yet the hope of mankind. Joseph endured unjust suffering and trials throughout his life, but his suffering points us to the One who has suffered in our place. Now we can face suffering and trials with hope because we know that God will work every part of our lives and every chapter of our stories for our good and His glory. We may not always understand, and the plan may not seem good in the moment, but there will come a day in this life or eternity that we will look back and see God's overwhelming faithfulness to His children. Joseph's story reminds us that our faithful God will not forsake us and that we can trust His plan even when it does not make sense to our finite minds.

In chapter 40, we once again see that the Lord is gifting Joseph through interpreting dreams. God provided this gift to Joseph, uses it to provide for him, and uses it to point back to His providence in Joseph's life. Do you find yourself using your God-given talents for the glory of God and edification of the church, or do you find that you use them for your own gain?

Joseph finds favor with the Pharaoh because of his ability to interpret dreams. How did Joseph's God-given talent testify to a lost world about the glory of God? Does your stewardship of God's gifts in your life testify to a lost world of God's goodness?

How did God use Joseph in slavery for His purposes? How does this comfort you to know that God does not let our difficult seasons in life go unused?

Genesis 43-46

God is sovereign. He is sovereign over everything that ever comes into our lives—including our suffering.

But God's sovereignty in our lives does not mean that trusting His plan is always easy. The path of obedience may be filled with sorrow and heartache, but it is always worth it to walk in obedience no matter our circumstances.

Joseph's brothers returned to Egypt, and the plot deepens as Joseph reveals his identity to his unsuspecting brothers. Joseph wept as he told his brothers who he was. Yet right in the midst of confessing his identity, he declares that though his brothers sold him into slavery, God had a plan all along. Joseph uses the words, "God sent me," and shows that what happened to him was all part of God's plan (Genesis 45:5-7). Even in Joseph's deep pain and rejection, he was able to see that God had a plan through it all and that he had not ended up in Egypt simply by the act of his brothers but by the providence of God. God had sent him, and God had gone with him. At the end of chapter 46, we see that Jacob and Joseph are reunited after years apart. Though we usually focus on the sorrow of Joseph in this situation, we can be assured that this was a painful part of Jacob's turbulent life. But through it all, God was faithful.

Joseph's story reminds us that we can be confident in the Lord and His plan, even through suffering. Though we do not understand, we can trust that His way is perfect (Psalm 18:30). We can trust that He works all things for the good of His children (Romans 8:28). God brings good out of the awful circumstances of our lives. He does not come up with a plan when things go badly; He had a plan from the beginning. He does not scramble to fix the mess we made but instead works every foreknown circumstance for our ultimate good. It is always for our good and His glory. In this same way, God brought good from the most heartbreaking moment of history. At the cross, Jesus bore the weight of our sin and suffered and died in our place. Our greatest good would come from His greatest suffering.

"Though we do not understand, we can trust that His way is perfect."

Joseph's very own family sells him into slavery. He is wrongfully thrown into prison. A famine is what brings Joseph's brothers to Egypt. How do all of these things testify and affirm what Paul says in Romans 8:28?

In Genesis 45:5, we see Joseph console his brothers. He assures them not to be worried about the sins they committed against him because God is using him powerfully to preserve the lives of his family. How does this encourage you in the knowledge that God's plan is good, even when we experience heartache?

Reread Genesis 45:5, and reflect on the depth of mercy that is found in what Joseph is saying. In what ways can you see God revealing glimpses of His great mercy toward us through Joseph's gestures?

Genesis 47-50

We have come to the end of the book of beginnings, and we see the family of Jacob settling in the land of Egypt.

The famine has come, and Joseph's faithfulness saves many people, including his own family. Jacob blesses his sons before his death, and we cannot help but be amazed at how God had chosen this ordinary and dysfunctional family to be His people. We even see a mention of the scepter not departing from Judah in Genesis 49:10. This line of Judah sees this promise confirmed later in the Davidic covenant (2 Samuel 7). This promise is also ultimately fulfilled in Jesus, who is the Lion of Judah and the One who will sit on David's throne (Revelation 5:5). The family is full of sin, suffering, struggle, and tragedy, and yet the Lord has called them His own. And not only did the Lord call them His own, but He chose them to be the ones from whom the Messiah would come.

Through all of the disasters, God had a great plan from the beginning. And He has a plan for each of us. In the situation of Joseph and so many in his family, we see that what some people meant for evil, God meant for good (Genesis 50:20). God's plan will always prevail. His plan is good. He is waiting and ready to redeem.

God's sovereign hand was on Joseph's life. The result of the suffering and rejection of Joseph would be God's good plan, and part of that good plan would be the saving of many people. Joseph is an illustration of Jesus for us. Jesus would face far greater suffering, and God would use that suffering to rescue and redeem the people He loves. In Joseph's story, people from around the world are saved from famine, but Jesus rescues many more from the grips of sin and death.

"Through all of the disasters, God had a great plan from the beginning."

Joseph's faithfulness to Pharaoh gives Israel a settling place for a time and preserves them. How does this encourage you in God's provision and plan?

In Genesis 50:15-21, we see yet again that Joseph heaps loads of kindness upon his brothers' heads. What are some practical ways you might be able to heap kindness upon those who revile against you?

We have come to the end of Genesis; what are some major themes that have emerged from this book? What do these major themes tell us about the nature of God and the nature of man?

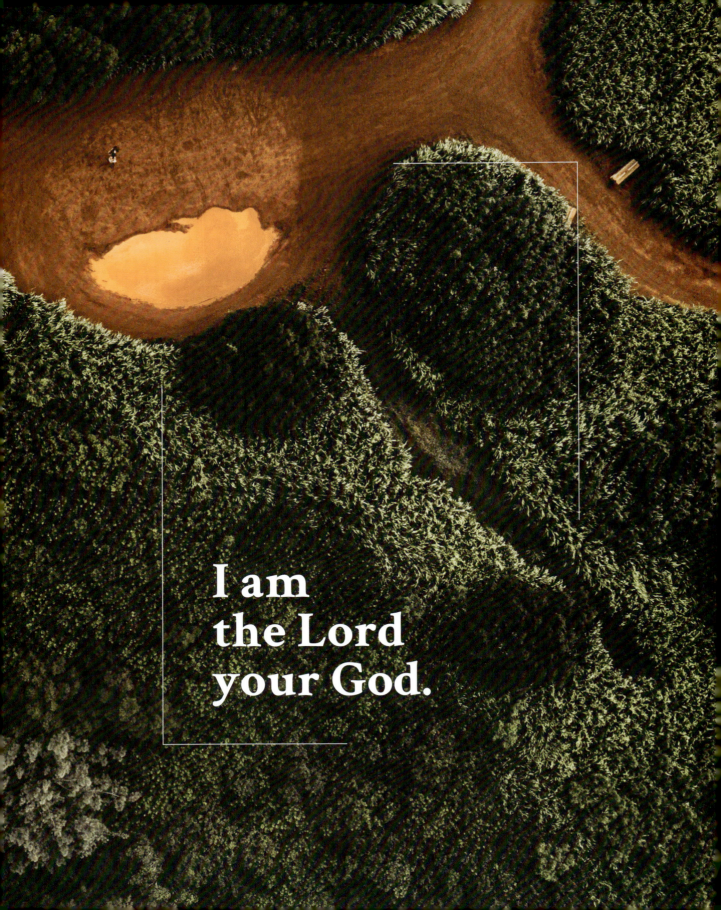

I am
the Lord
your God.

Exodus

GENRE: Law, Historical Narrative

AUTHOR / DATE WRITTEN

Moses • c. 1440-1400 BC

MAJOR THEMES —— Deliverance from Slavery, Rebellion Against God, Covenant Faithfulness

KEY WORDS —— Covenant, Faithfulness, Provision

KEY VERSE

EXODUS 20:2

I am the Lord your God, who brought you out of the land of Egypt, out of the place of slavery.

Exodus 1-3

The book of Exodus begins with reminders of God's faithfulness.

God's promises to Abraham about a nation of descendants were coming to pass. We learn that a new king came to power who does not know Joseph. The children of Israel had multiplied, and the Egyptians were getting worried. As a solution, Pharaoh decided to direct the Hebrew midwives to kill all male babies at birth. However, these courageous women disregarded the king and did what was right. Pharaoh formed a ruthless plan to squash the people of God, but no scheme of man can thwart the sovereign plan of God. The family of Abraham would not be annihilated because this is the family through which the promised Redeemer would come.

Chapter 2 shifts our attention to one Hebrew son, and the text shows Moses is born, and to save his life, his mother places him in a basket in the river. He is rescued out of a basket in the river by Pharaoh's daughter. Moses is another person whose life points us to Jesus. The man who becomes the rescuer of a nation points to the far greater rescuer who would come to all who believe.

The next couple of chapters give us a rush of information. Moses grows up, commits a horrible crime, flees to Midian, and then meets God at the burning bush. God had indeed heard, seen, and known the plight of His children, and now He comes and equips Moses to be the chosen deliverer (Exodus 3:7-8). God is the great I AM and the great deliverer. God had come to rescue the ones who He loved. He does the same for us. He always shows up at just the right moment to deliver His children. He does not leave us hopeless. He hears, sees, knows—and He will come.

The greatest fulfillment of God coming to the aid of His people is in Jesus Himself. John 1:14 tells us that the Word became flesh and dwelt among us. He came down. God, wrapped in flesh, came as a humble baby to be our rescuer and redeemer. Our Emmanuel came to save. So as we read the story of Moses, our hearts point to the One who Moses spoke of. John 5:46 reminds us that every word of Scripture, including the words of Moses, point to Jesus.

At the start of Exodus, we see the fruition of God's covenant with Abraham—
that his offspring would be numerous. However, this causes the Egyptians to
panic. Take a moment, and think about how the midwives were used by God as a
tangible way to make His promises come to fruition. In what ways are you being
used by God so that His promises are coming to fruition?

The first instance of deliverance that we see in this book is through
Moses's miraculous survival of drifting in a river, in a wicker basket,
surrounded by obstacles. How does this bolster your confidence in God
that He will always deliver you?

In Exodus 3:14-15, we see that God refers to Himself as "I AM WHO I AM" and
that this is how He should be remembered in every generation. Take a moment
to reflect on the power of this name and what it means.

Exodus 4-6

Instead of focusing on God's power, Moses focuses on his weakness. He does not feel equipped to be the deliverer. He lists out all of the reasons that he was not qualified. Moses feared man more than he feared God, but God had called him to lead the people, and God would equip him. It is easy for us to focus on the failings of Moses to trust God as he lists out all of the reasons he is not qualified. But in this passage, we also see an example of stumbling faith. God is not looking for us to have it all together. He is looking for obedience and surrender. That is how God uses us to build His kingdom.

Despite the shortcomings or limitations that Moses thinks he has, he returned to Egypt. Moses and Aaron tell the people all God had said, and the people believe and worship the Lord because He has heard their cries for deliverance. It is interesting to note that this worship precedes their deliverance. They did not worship because they had gotten what they wanted; they worshiped God for who He was and trusted He could do what He had promised to do. Though deliverance had been promised, the road ahead would not be easy.

Pharaoh was not sympathetic to the peril of the Hebrews or to the message from the Lord. Instead of releasing the children of Israel, he made their work even harder. The people who had just cheered on Moses and Aaron are now angry and discouraged. At the end of chapter 5, we even see Moses crying out to God in despair. But the Lord speaks to Moses and reminds him of who He is. He is the great I AM. He hears the sorrows of His people, and He remembers His covenant. He has not forgotten His people. No matter how bad our circumstances or how bad things seem to be, we can always trust the Lord because of who He is. His character shows us that we can be confident in Him. He will never fail His people. He is steadfast and true. He is for us. Is there any greater example of God seeing the need of His people and keeping His covenant than Jesus Himself? God will not forsake us. The cross stands as a monument to His covenant-keeping love for His people.

"We can always trust the Lord because of who He is."

Moses fears man, in part, because he knew his insecurities. Are your insecurities getting in the way of your obedience to the Lord? How can learning about the ways that God used Moses bolster your confidence in God above your fleshly weaknesses?

Reread Exodus 5:8-9. Pharaoh knows that it is easy to fix our gaze on busyness rather than on God. Is your gaze fixed on God despite the busyness of life? Does Satan prevail when he attempts to distract you from godly priorities?

In Exodus 6:6-9, we see another promise from God to His people. How do these continual reaffirmations of God's promises expand your understanding of who God is?

Exodus 7-9

God sent Moses and Aaron into Egypt to say what He would tell them to say and do what He would tell them to do.

God was at work, and His plan was one of deliverance and redemption for His people. God declared that all of Egypt would know that He was the Lord. These chapters cover some of the plagues that would come about as a result of Pharaoh's refusal to heed the commands of God. These judgments from the Lord teach the people and us that all creation is under the Lord's power. Each of the plagues corresponds with an idol the Egyptians worshiped. And by sending the plagues, God shows that there is no other god besides Him. The intricate control of our God over every aspect of the world is a stunning reminder of how we can trust Him. There is not a single thing outside of the power and control of our God.

But these stunning judgments are also a magnificent display of God's mercy. Each plague is a chance to repent. They call to repentance as they remind us that God is sovereign over every idol. The plagues also show Pharaoh that he is not in control. God was revealing His power, His majesty, and Himself through the plagues, and the result was that Pharaoh's heart was hardened. When a person is brought face to face with who God is, our sinful nature will push against Him. Throughout these chapters, we see that Pharaoh hardened his heart and that God hardened Pharaoh's heart. This can be a confusing concept. But, Romans 9:14-18 sheds some light on this passage. There, we see that the purpose of the hardening of Pharaoh's heart was so God's name would be proclaimed throughout the earth. The grace of God is the only thing that can melt a heart of stone. We can be assured that apart from divine intervention of grace, our hearts will be hardened. But the grace of God is our hope. We can always trust in God's sovereignty and know that He will always do what is right.

The Lord is sovereign over the world and our lives. God was preparing for the deliverance of His people. In doing so, He was showing the Egyptians and Hebrews His power and majesty. The plagues remind us of God's amazing power over all things and His steadfast love and mercy that He extends time and time again.

"God is our hope."

How does the power of God displayed through the plagues grow your admiration for Him?

How does this grow your fear and reverence of Him?

Each plague was directed specifically at idol worship. How does this give a new meaning to Moses asking Pharaoh to "Let my people go" in Exodus 9:1?

Exodus 10-12

The plagues were coming to a close, and the last plague was drawing near.

Every plague had been another opportunity to repent, but each one was met only with the hardness of heart. The day had finally come—the day that would change everything. With this final plague, the firstborn sons would die, but God had made a way of deliverance. God directs the Hebrews to use the blood of spotless lambs to save their firstborn sons. This story points us to Jesus, our spotless Lamb. Jesus is our Passover Lamb.

It is interesting to see that in Exodus 12:17, God speaks of how they will remember this day as the day they were delivered from Egypt. And God speaks those words before they are even delivered. Because in the hands of our sovereign God, our victory is sure. He will deliver us. He will do what He has promised to do. And in Exodus 12:31, the Hebrews are set free. In fact, in Exodus 12:36, we learn that the Lord had given this enslaved multitude of people so much favor with the Egyptians that the Egyptians sent them out with great wealth, which God would eventually use for His tabernacle. To the people of Egypt, this was a great multitude of slaves, but in the eyes of God, these were His chosen and set apart people. And God will never fail His people.

Passover teaches us about substitutionary atonement. Which means that either the Lamb, Jesus, dies, or we die (2 Corinthians 5:21). Jesus is our door and deliverer. He is the Lamb. For thousands of years, the Passover would be celebrated in remembrance of their deliverance. However, the Passover also serves to point to the Messiah, as John 5:46 reminds us that Moses was talking about Jesus when talking about the Passover lamb. We live because the firstborn Son of God has died in our place. This story is not just the story of the Israelites—it is our story as well. Egypt is the picture of sin and the world, and just like the Hebrews needed deliverance, we needed deliverance too. And at just the right time, God rescued us with the blood of the firstborn (Romans 5:6). Passover was a picture of the Promised One, the true deliverer, for whom Israel yearned. And now the Passover is a picture that reminds us of all Jesus did for us when He delivered us from the power of sin and death. He has come, and He has rescued us at just the right time. He is never late to fulfill His promises. He is the faithful One. And if He is faithful in salvation, we know that we can trust Him with every moment of our lives.

"Jesus is our door and deliverer. He is the Lamb."

QUESTIONS

There were ten plagues total—each a chance for repentance. What does this tell us about God's long-suffering nature toward us?

Spend some additional time dwelling on the spotless Lamb. Reflect on what this symbolized to the Israelites during this tenth plague, and dwell on what it means to us now.

With these plagues being direct attacks on the idol worship of the day, take a moment to reflect on the ways that you are tempted into idol worship in your own life.

Exodus 13-15

But the Lord made His presence clear from the start. A cloud by day and a pillar of fire by night is God's way of showing His people that He is with them and that He will lead them. And though they had just been delivered, the Red Sea was a place that He would deliver them again. The people waited hopelessly on the shore of the Red Sea with the enemy fast approaching when Moses told the people to be still and see the salvation of the Lord. It is the Lord who would fight for them (Exodus 14:14). The Lord did fight for them that day, and they walked through the Red Sea on dry land with walls of water surrounding them that would soon crash down on their enemies.

A song of worship is the fitting response of the people to the deliverance that they had just experienced. Chapter 15 includes the song of Moses, and it is a song of worship and praise to God for who He is and what He has done. He had done what no one else could do. He is worthy of praise. At the end of chapter 15, the people who had just sung in worship grumble because they have no water to drink. Yet God faithfully provided for their need and then led them to a place of abundance after their momentary doubt. It may seem silly to us that the people doubted in the same chapter that they praised God for miraculous deliverance, but we are often quick to do the same. We see His care for us and then worry about the smallest details of our lives as if He is not powerful enough to provide.

He makes a way when there seems to be no way. He does that by parting the Red Sea, providing water, and He did the same thing for us in salvation. He made a way for us to be justified when our sin separated us from God. And whatever we are facing in our lives, He can make a way. We can trust Him completely. We can be still and know that He is God and that we are not. We can trust His plan, and we can trust His heart.

"He makes a way when there seems to be no way."

We see in chapter 13 that God provides a pillar of cloud by day and a pillar of fire by night to direct the wandering Israelites. Today, we have the very Word of God to direct us in navigating life. Do you treat your Scripture reading with such reverence?

In Exodus 14:17-18, God says, "I will receive glory by means of Pharaoh, all his army, and his chariots and horsemen. The Egyptians will know that I am the Lord when I receive glory through Pharaoh, his chariots, and his horsemen." Spend some additional time thinking about how God receives glory from the display of justice in both ancient and modern times.

The Israelites were delivered from Pharaoh's advancements, and they sang praises to God. Take some time to dwell on how worshiping God through music allows us to delight in Him in a unique way. How does this encourage you to worship the Lord more fully?

Exodus 16-18

The people saw the powerful deliverance of God, and yet they still grumbled and did not trust.

Whatever they needed, the Lord had provided, but still, they questioned His love and His plan. When they were thirsty, He provided water. When they were hungry, He provided manna. God rained bread from heaven to meet their needs. The manna came daily. It is a sweet reminder of our daily need for the Lord and His Word. It reminds us that we are not self-sufficient. We need Him. We need Him every single day. The manna also reminds us of His faithfulness. The Lord provided manna every single day without fail for forty years. But more importantly, this bread from heaven points us to the true bread from heaven. Jesus spoke of this story in John 6:22-59 when He declared He is the Bread of Life.

He will never fail His people. He will always provide just what they need. He provides for us, and He also teaches us to trust Him. Even with all of the provisions they had experienced, the people still complained. Chapter 17 brings another beautiful picture of Jesus right in the midst of their complaining. Jesus is the rock that was struck so that we might have life (1 Corinthians 10:4), and now from Him pours out streams of living water. In the same passage in John 6, in which Jesus proclaimed that He was the Bread of Life, He also tells us that He is the Living Water and that those who come to Him will never thirst (John 6:35). Jesus is the only one who can quench our thirsty souls. We can always trust the Lord to provide. From daily provision to the Rock of our salvation—He is our provider.

Chapter 18 closes today's reading with a reminder of how God uses the testimonies of His people. Moses's father-in-law, Jethro, heard the testimony of Moses about God's faithful deliverance, and he was converted. Though our stories have no power to save other people, they do point those around us to the only One with the power to save. Chapter after chapter, we see that the testimony of the Word of God points to Jesus, who is our Savior. He is the Bread of Life, the Rock struck for our salvation, and the living water.

"The testimony of the Word of God points to Jesus, who is our Savior."

QUESTIONS

Each day the Lord faithfully provided food to last the Israelites for the day, and whatever was stored up for the next day became spoiled. How does this passage expand your understanding of Matthew 6:34?

In Exodus 17:3, we see how quickly the Israelites forget that the Lord has faithfully provided for them. Do you find yourself often forgetting that God will faithfully provide for you too?

In chapter 18, Jethro rejoices on account of hearing the good things that the Lord had done for Israel. Think of some ways you can be intentionally rejoicing with believers in your church, country, or around the world because of the good things the Lord is doing.

Exodus 19-21

We find ourselves at the base of Mt. Sinai. God is about to give the law—a law that will point toward the people's need for a redeemer and establish Israel as a nation.

But the purpose of the law is not for the people to earn the love of God—He already loves them. Exodus 19:4 shows us that God has rescued them from Egypt for Himself and makes them His treasured possession. God did not give the people the law as a condition of their redemption out of Egypt. He redeemed them, and then He gave them standards for holiness. It is another simple reminder that we cannot earn our redemption. We can only rest in His saving grace.

The law serves to show the people their need for the promised Messiah. When the people see their weakness, they are reminded of their need for a Savior. The law also reveals God's character and points to Jesus, who would be the one to fulfill it. The law points out our sin and weakness and looks forward to Jesus, who does what we could not do. In Jesus's life, He perfectly and completely fulfills the requirements of the law that we could never fulfill for ourselves. In His death, He became our atoning sacrifice. And in His resurrection, He proved that death and sin do not have power over Him.

Even the law that we could never live up to was a gift of grace. It serves to point us to Jesus, who makes everything right. The law shows us who we are, but more importantly, it shows us who He is. He is the answer. The law draws our hearts to worship the God who comes to rescue and redeem us as His people. In Exodus 19:4, we learned that God had redeemed the people to be His own, and the same is true for us. We have been redeemed to be His and to worship Him (1 Peter 2:9). Now our lives are lived as an overflow of worship to the One who has given everything for us.

"We cannot earn our redemption. We can only rest in His saving grace."

In chapter 19, we see the strict instructions Moses has to ensure that no one dies if they see God. What does this chapter teach us about God's holiness and immeasurable glory?

As you read the Ten Commandments, think about Matthew 22:36-40. How does coupling these verses together expand your understanding of both passages?

Spend some time reflecting on the law. How does reading through these ordinances highlight your shortcomings as a human? Does this grow your affections for Christ being completely perfect?

Exodus 22-24

These chapters continue with God giving more laws to establish the nation and bring order to the people.

The chapters overflow with laws applying to a variety of areas in life. Yet, one thing is clear from these laws put in place by God—He cares for His people. He cares for the poor, the marginalized, and the oppressed. He wants justice to reign because He is a God of justice. The law is a call to holiness—it establishes the standard of what is right and true. It points us to Jesus, who will be the only one to fulfill it. These passages also give the people the hope of Canaan, the Promised Land where they would dwell. And in all of this, it is clear that God is setting a people apart for Himself.

At the confirmation of the covenant, Moses came before the people, and the people promise that they will "do everything that the Lord has commanded" (Exodus 24:3). The people making the promise were likely woefully unaware of their inability to, in their own strength, fulfill the law set before them. Blood is then sprinkled on the altar and on the people. It may not seem to make sense at first, but we must remember that without the shedding of blood, there is no remission of sins (Hebrews 9:22). In the Passover, God showed mercy in passing over His people when He saw the blood (Exodus 12:13), and this reminds us of that same truth. The covenant was formed, but it was just a foreshadowing of a better covenant that was to come. This covenant serves to point our hearts toward Jesus, who came to cover us in His blood, providing us with His grace, mercy, and unfailing love. This covenant ceremony, when the people are covered in the blood of oxen, makes us long for the new and better covenant in which our sins are washed white with the blood of the spotless Lamb of God.

God knows His people. He knew the nation of Israel. And He knows us. He knows that we will make promises and that we will fail, but He never fails. This passage reminds us of God's mercy, grace, and steadfast love for His own. Though we have no power to keep the law in our own strength, Jesus would come and perfectly keep the law in our place.

"God knows His people."

56

QUESTIONS

How do these passages on the law expand your understanding of the necessity of Jesus coming to earth as a perfect man?

Spend some time thinking through the imagery and symbolism of blood and sacrifice in Genesis through Exodus—does this give you a better understanding of what the sacrifice of Jesus on the cross means?

Dwell on the fact that God has given us a way to be reconciled to Him through the sacrifice of His Son. What does this tell you about the character of God?

Exodus 25-27

Intro statement The tabernacle points us to Jesus. In Hebrews 10:1, the author of Hebrews speaks of how the law was just a shadow of what was to come.

And as we look at the tabernacle, we can see how every detail was pointing to the message of the gospel and Jesus. Each detail was planned by God as a picture to point to Jesus.

The tabernacle reminds us that God wants to dwell with His people (John 1:14). The ark of the covenant and mercy seat remind us that God does not only deal with us by the law but by His mercy and grace. We look to the cross, the true and better mercy seat, where our substitution was made. The table of bread reminds us that Jesus is the Bread of Life (John 6:35). The golden lampstand points to Him being the Light of the World (John 8:12). There was a curtain between the Holy place and the rest of the tabernacle that represented the separation between God and man. When Jesus died on the cross, that curtain was torn to show that we are no longer separated but have open access to the Lord (Matthew 27:51). We have access to God because of Jesus and His death on the cross. The bronze altar was a picture of substitution and the cross. Sin had a price, but there was a sacrifice that would pay the price for us. The Hebrew people only knew of the temporary sacrifice of a lamb, but we know of the final and once for all sacrifice of Jesus (Romans 6:10, Hebrews 10:12, Hebrews 10:14). Jesus is the gate and the only way to enter God's presence. Every piece of furniture and every detail proclaim the truth that Jesus saves.

Jesus has done what we could never do. The God who longed to dwell with His people would come in the body of Jesus to dwell, or tabernacle, among them. And now, the tabernacle is also a picture of the people of God. God dwells with us and in us now. We must stand in awe as we look at the tabernacle with each piece as a picture of the redemption that only Jesus can bring. We also fix our gaze to the future as we await the return of Jesus and the day that we will dwell with Him in fullness and experience the glory of His presence before us. On that day, there will be no need for a temple or a tabernacle because God will dwell with His people forever (Revelation 21-22). So we fix our gaze on Jesus. We look back at every picture that pointed toward Him, and we await His return.

"Jesus has done what we could never do."

In Exodus 25:2, we see that God wanted willing givers to sacrifice to Him.
What are some ways you find yourself willing to sacrifice to God?
What are some ways you find yourself unwilling to sacrifice?

What can we learn about God by the intricacies He demanded
in the tabernacle?

In Exodus 27:8, we see very specific instructions for the construction
of the tabernacle. What do we learn about God from the exactness
of the instructions He gave?

Exodus 28-30

In these chapters, we are introduced to the priests.

We see their garments, their consecration, and their sacrifices, but the priesthood was always meant to point to Jesus. He is our Great High Priest. It also points forward to the priesthood of believers and the truth that under Jesus who is our High Priest, we can come boldly before our God. Jesus would fulfill and perfect the picture. The priests offered sacrifices continually, but Jesus would be the once for all sacrifice for the sins of His people. The priests wore white robes that would be stained with the blood of the sacrifices. Someday the children of God who have been washed in the blood of the Lamb will wear robes of white. This is only made possible because of the finished work of Christ and His shed blood on the cross of Calvary.

Chapter 30 shows the last items of the tabernacle, and each one points to Jesus. The altar of incense represents prayer going up before God as a sweet aroma. The prayers of the people of God still ascend to heaven as a sweet aroma to God. The next item is the bronze basin which is where the priests would wash before entering God's presence. In the same way, we also have been washed. We have been washed in the blood of Jesus, and we can enter His presence because we have been made clean. Our sins have been washed white in the blood of the Lamb who has come to take away the sins of His people. In the oil and incense, we are reminded that though we were once marked and covered in the smell of sin and death, we now have the aroma of Christ (2 Corinthians 2:15). Each element points to Jesus and reminds us of the beauty of who He is.

We are His children who now dwell in the presence of our God because of what Jesus has done on the cross. His blood was shed for our sins. He is our perfect substitution. He has washed us and made us new so that we can praise Him forever.

"He has washed us and made us new so that we can praise Him forever."

In Exodus 28:21, we see that the twelve stones required in the priest's breast piece represent the twelve names of Israel's sons. What other symbolism do you see that appears in the priestly garments?

Chapter 29 is all about consecration. What does this inform us about God's concern for our holiness?

In the same way, how does the consecration of the priest deepen your understanding of Christ's perfection?

Exodus 31-33

Throughout these pages of Scripture, we get a glimpse of God and His people.

On the mountaintop, the Lord was speaking to Moses about the necessity of Sabbath rest. While at the base of the mountain, the people and Aaron were building a golden calf. The people do not trust the Lord despite all that He had done for them. They wanted to worship a god of their creation, a god that they could see. They did not want to wait on the Lord; they wanted something in front of their eyes that they could worship. And Aaron went along with their plan and then tried to shift the blame for his sin onto others. It is easy to be disgusted by their actions, but when we look at our own hearts, we know that there are times we want God to do things the way that we want them done. We want Him to do what we think is best. And, like Aaron, we are quick to shift the blame of our sin to those around us. Yet, God is loving and patient with us and always seeking to bring us back to Himself.

In these chapters, we also get a glimpse into the sweet relationship between Moses and the Lord. Exodus 33:11 shows us that God speaks to Moses as a man speaks to his friend. It is here that Moses pleas for God's presence. Moses begs for one glimpse of God's glory. Moses knows that he cannot do this without the Lord, so He tells the Lord in desperation that he cannot go on without the Lord. God was going to give His people the Promised Land without His presence. Yet Moses knew that the Promised Land would be empty without the presence of God.

The rest God promised for His people is rest that can be fully found in Jesus alone. Moses saw a glimpse of God's character, and we now see it in Jesus, who came to dwell with us. Over and over in the passage, Moses refers to the favor of the Lord, and this is His grace. We experience God's grace for us through the finished work of Christ. Let us have hearts like Moses that see our great need for the Lord. We need His presence as He knows us by name, calls us His own, and gives us Himself. Our God is the only One who will satisfy.

"The rest God promised for His people is rest that can be fully found in Jesus alone."

Exodus 31:1-6 shows that God provides and calls skilled workers. What are some ways that God is leading you to use your gifts within the church?

As you think about the golden calf that the Israelites fashioned, also think about the idols you might have built up in your own heart. How can we learn from the Israelites in their horrible mistake?

We have seen great portraits of God as holy in the book of Exodus, and then we read Exodus 33:11 and see that God speaks to Moses as a man speaks to his friend. How does this grow your understanding of the character of God?

Exodus 34-36

If you have ever wanted to know who God is, you will see here precisely who He is as He describes Himself to Moses.

He is merciful and gracious. He is slow to anger and abounding in steadfast love and faithfulness. He is the God of covenants. He will never forget the covenant that He makes with His people. He is a God who does not ignore sin—and that is the point of the cross. He did not ignore our sin; He paid for it. Our sin, which could not be ignored, was placed on Jesus, who absorbed the wrath of God in our place. The face of Moses shines after he sees God's glory, and we also should shine before others (2 Corinthians 3-4). A glimpse of the character and person of God transforms us from one degree of glory to another. The shining face of Moses should remind us that we long for the world to see God in us. We cannot meet with God and not be changed forever.

When the building of the tabernacle begins, the people come with their contributions and their skills to help in the work. Every person had something to bring to contribute to the work of building a dwelling place for God. In the same way, God has given us all unique gifts and skills to help serve each other and the Lord (Romans 12:4-8, I Corinthians 12:12-30). He has given us everything that we need to serve Him.

Moses saw a glimpse of God's glory as he hid behind a rock, but when Jesus came, we see the glory of God embodied in Jesus. In Jesus, God came full of grace and truth to dwell with man and showed us the glory of God (John 1:14). If we want to know who God is, we can look to Christ. As we look to Jesus and the cross, we are transformed into the image of Jesus, who is the glorious one.

"He did not ignore our sin; He paid for it."

Pay close attention to Exodus 34:4-7 as God proclaims His character to Moses. Are there parts of God's character that you tend to emphasize more than others? Reflect on how to have a balanced and true view of God's character.

In Exodus 34:28, we see that Moses was alone with the Lord for forty days and forty nights without food or water. He had no friends with him and no food or water, yet he still returned from his meeting glowing from what he now had seen of the Lord. What does this imply about God's sufficiency for us?

There was so much material given toward the building of the tabernacle that Moses had to give an order for people to stop offering their belongings. What does this say about the necessity for generosity in the church and how God uses His people's resources in the church to provide?

Exodus 37-40

The book of Exodus concludes with the final construction of the tabernacle. And we see that each piece points to Jesus.

God had promised the people that they would leave Egypt and worship in the wilderness, and here that promise is fulfilled. In Exodus 29:43-46, God declared that He had brought the children of Israel out of Egypt to dwell with them. In the immediate sense, God dwells with them right here in the midst of their wilderness wanderings in the tabernacle. However, this promise's true and better fulfillment comes generations later when Jesus dwells with His people on earth. Immanuel, God with us, is the greatest fulfillment of this promise.

The word "tabernacle" means "dwelling place," and the end of chapter forty shows that God comes to dwell in the tabernacle. The tabernacle is one temporary solution in a list of many momentary solutions for God's dwelling place. Throughout Scripture, we see God dwell in Eden, the tabernacle, the temple, in Jesus, and in the church. In the New Testament, God dwells with man through the person of Jesus (John 1:14). Someday we will see the new heaven where God will dwell with man forever in perfect communion (Revelation 21). On that day, there will be no need for a tabernacle or temple because God will be with us.

Right now, the church is the temple of God (1 Corinthians 6:19), and the picture is beautiful but not perfect because of sin. Someday everything will be made perfect, and the dwelling place of God will be with man (Revelation 21:3). He will make everything new. There will be no more tears or pain. We will worship Him with no temple (Revelation 21:22) because He will be in our midst. And the years of wilderness wandering will be in the past as we dwell with Him forever.

"He will make everything new."

Take a moment to reflect on the dwelling places of God. What can we learn about God through His desire to dwell near us?

Now think of the intricacies of the tabernacle as God's dwelling place. What can we learn about the intricacies God has built into our bodies through the understanding that the Holy Spirit now dwells in us?

Reflect on what it might have looked like to see the glory of the Lord filling the tabernacle as described in Exodus 40:34. In what ways do we get to see the glory of the Lord throughout the world today?

I have
set you
apart.

Leviticus

GENRE: Law, Historical Narrative

AUTHOR / DATE WRITTEN

Moses • c. 1440-1400 BC

MAJOR THEMES — Holiness of God, Necessity of Sacrifice for Man's Fallen Nature

KEY WORDS — Sacrifice, Priesthood, Purity, Holiness

KEY VERSE

LEVITICUS 20:26

You are to be holy to me because I, the Lord, am holy, and I have set you apart from the nations to be mine.

Leviticus 1-3

The book of Leviticus starts right where Exodus left off — in the tabernacle.

The Lord speaks to Moses from the dwelling place, which is something we will see throughout the book. In this book, we will learn about the law, sacrifice, and the holiness that God requires. However, in all of this, we will also see that this book constantly points us to Jesus.

These first chapters give instructions for sacrifice. Several phrases are key and repeated often throughout the book. We learn the sacrifice must be without blemish and that the sacrifice is a pleasing aroma to the Lord. We are also introduced to the concept of atonement.

Jesus is the Lamb without blemish who would be sacrificed for us (1 Peter 1:19, Hebrews 9:14, Hebrews 10:8-10). Since the fall, all of humanity has been infected with sin and in need of a perfect sacrifice. The sacrifices we learn about in Leviticus call for a sacrifice without blemish. This points us to Jesus, who is our perfect sacrifice. He is also our atoning sacrifice and the substitution for us (1 John 2:2, 1 Peter 2:24, 2 Corinthians 5:21). So, in short, atonement is Jesus Christ offering Himself as a sacrifice so that God and mankind can be reconciled. The penalty of our sin is a weight we could never bear, but Jesus bore the punishment of His people on the cross. It is there that His blood washes clean the stain of our sin. The sacrifice of Jesus is a pleasing aroma to the Lord, and because of what Jesus has done, He has made us a sweet aroma to the Lord as well (Ephesians 5:2, 2 Corinthians 2:15). Our sin is overwhelmed with the stench of death, but the sacrifice of Jesus is a pleasing aroma.

The imagery of a book like Leviticus may seem shocking to us at first, but the imagery is rich and beautiful. It shows us the consequences and penalty of our sin and points us to the perfect sacrifice. The first few chapters of Leviticus are a reminder that the Bible is a story of redemption that points to Jesus in every verse, on every page of Scripture.

"The Bible is a story of redemption that points to Jesus in every verse, on every page of Scripture."

What repeated words did you notice in these chapters?

Considering the phrase "without blemish" is repeatedly used in describing an appropriate sacrifice to the Lord, how does this deepen your understanding of Christ being the perfect sacrifice to atone for our sins?

What are some ways that your understanding of Jesus Christ's sacrifice has been deepened through understanding the tabernacle and sacrifices described in Exodus and Leviticus?

Leviticus 4-6

The book of Leviticus continues to give detailed instructions for all of the different types of sacrifices that needed to be made.

And though the concept of offering sacrifices seems so bloody and foreign to us, it is important to see that these all point to Jesus, who is the greater sacrifice. Leviticus reminds us of the weight of our sin. Sin makes things messy. Sin always costs something. Sin always leads to death.

We see several words and concepts repeated in these chapters, pointing our attention to Jesus just as in the first chapters of this book. The priests offer sacrifices to make atonement for sin, and forgiveness is granted. The people also needed someone to make sacrifices and offerings to God, which the priests did. There was one high priest who would yearly enter the holy of holies to make atonement sacrifices on behalf of God's people. Here we are given a reminder of how these difficult laws are to fulfill. And yet we know Jesus is our high priest and our atoning sacrifice. Forgiveness is found only in Him. And He is the one who goes to God on our behalf and clothes us in His righteousness so that we can come boldly to God (Hebrews 4:16). The blood of these animals would temporarily atone for the sins of the people, but it would be the blood of Jesus that would be the once for all atonement that we desperately need.

Over and over, we see the concept of substitution—the innocent paying the price for the guilty. For hundreds of years, the innocent animals would pay for sin, but there would come a day when Jesus would be the greater fulfillment. He would do what the animals could never do. Sacrifice after sacrifice would be made, but those sacrifices would never last because they were imperfect. But the perfect sacrifice of Jesus is once and for all. The sacrifice of Jesus gives all believers access to God. One sacrifice changes everything.

"The perfect sacrifice of Jesus is once and for all."

In Leviticus 4:27-28, we see that even unintentional sins require an atoning sacrifice. What does this teach you about the seriousness of sin?

In Leviticus 5:1, we see that we bear responsibility for sin that we know about and do not report. How does this shape the way you think about your sin? How does it impact the way you view sin in the lives of your brothers and sisters in Christ?

In chapter 6, we see that the fire is to burn on the altar at all times. What does this tell us about the graciousness and availability that we have with God?

Leviticus 7-9

Every sacrifice has a cost.

The sacrifices in the book of Leviticus were costly to the animals that were sacrificed, and they were costly to the person making the sacrifice. The best animal of the herd must be put on the altar as payment for the sin of the offender. These required, spotless animals were often financially costly to the people who were required to bring their sacrifices. Sacrifices could include long journeys and time away, but the result was that sin was covered. In the same way, the sacrifice of Jesus cost Him everything. His sacrifice is a reminder to us of just how much we have to be thankful for. We are thankful that we do not have to offer the sacrifices seen here in Leviticus, and we are thankful that He is our perfect once and for all sacrifice who has taken on the punishment of our sin in our place.

In these chapters, we learn more about the priesthood and how they must be set apart. It points us to Jesus, who is our Great High Priest, and it is also a stunning reminder that now every believer is called to be a priest as 1 Peter 2:9 reminds us. Because of the sacrifice of Jesus, we can come freely before the Lord. We can come confessing sin, we can come in thanksgiving for all that He has done, and we can come in prayer and relationship because of the substitutionary atonement of Jesus.

We continue to feel the weight of sin and the glory of the One who has paid the price in our place. Leviticus should compel us to worship God for who He is and all that He has done for us. Our sin and our shame are gone because of what He has done. The need for continual sacrifice has passed because He has made everything right. He is our perfect Lamb without blemish, who provided perfect atonement and declared us forgiven. He has done what we could not do. He has made every wrong right, and He has called us His own.

"We continue to feel the weight of sin and the glory of the One who has paid the price in our place."

Leviticus 7:12 describes how not all sacrifices are atonement but that there are also sacrifices made of thanksgiving. How does this grow your understanding of how we are to worship God?

Knowing that these sacrifices require the death of something innocent, how can you better understand dying to yourself as described in Galatians 2:20?

As you read about the priesthood in chapter 9, how does your understanding of Jesus as the Great High Priest deepen? See Hebrews 7:11-26.

Leviticus 10-12

"Clean" and "unclean." "Holy" and "unholy." Throughout the book of Leviticus and the Old Testament, we see these words.

They are some of the most prominent themes that we find in the books of the Law. At first, they seem to reference the ceremonial aspects of the Old Testament and the law given to the people, but as the Old Testament progresses, we see that it is not just the outside that God desires to make clean. In Psalms, we see David asking God to cleanse his heart (Psalm 51:2, Psalm 51:10). God is concerned with our holiness, and He is concerned with our hearts. These chapters that call us to holiness remind us that we can never measure up to the standard of God's perfection on our own. They point us to our need for someone to make us clean. As foreshadowed in the old covenant ceremony, the Law points us to the only One who can make us clean within.

The entire Old Testament is looking forward to the person who can cleanse us within. Over and over in the New Testament, we are reminded that Jesus is the answer, and He is the one who has cleansed us (Hebrews 1:3, 1 John 1:7, Titus 3:5, 1 Corinthians 6:11, John 15:3). When Jesus came to earth, He lived the perfect life that we could not live on our own, and He died the death that we deserved. He fulfilled the law in our place. The laws that pointed us to Him have been perfectly fulfilled in Him.

We no longer need to look ahead for this cleansing because Jesus has already come. If we are His children, He has cleansed us from our sin. When God looks at us, He sees the righteousness of Jesus in the place of our sin. We are made clean because of who He is. And now we can walk in the holiness that comes from within as a response for all that He has done for us.

"When God looks at us, He sees the righteousness of Jesus in the place of our sin."

Continue to think about the juxtapositions of "clean" and "unclean." How can you better understand both the condition of man and the character of God by contemplating these words?

Nadab and Abihu were consumed by fire from the Lord because they presented unauthorized fire before the Lord. What does this tell you about the holiness of God? What does this tell you about the importance of obedience to God's commands?

How does the purification ritual for touching dead animals, as described in chapter 11, grow your understanding of both God's holiness and the way that sin and death taint us?

Leviticus 13-15

In these chapters, we continue to think about "clean" and "unclean," "holy" and "unholy."

And these laws form vivid pictures in our minds that point us to Jesus. The disease of leprosy is found throughout Scripture. It is a disease that we do not often encounter in today's culture, but it has a rich symbolism throughout Scripture. This passage in Leviticus deals with laws pertaining to this terrible disease.

Leprosy represents sin—the disease that affects all of us. The disease of sin entered the world at the fall and has wreaked havoc on our world ever since. Just as leprosy separated a person from society, sin separates us from God. We are sick with sin. We are infected by it. And even one speck of sin makes us completely unclean in the sight of a holy, righteous, and perfect God. Just as the smallest spot of leprosy was enough to separate a person from their community, the smallest amount of sin separates us from a holy God.

In the New Testament, Jesus not only heals lepers, but He also reaches out and touches them. Jesus is the answer to the problem of sin that is in all of us. As the leper needed to be washed (Leviticus 14:4-8), we have been washed by Jesus, and we are now clean before Him (1 Corinthians 6:11). We have been cleansed by the blood of Jesus (1 John 1:7). We have been set free and redeemed because of Jesus. We look to the cross as the remedy for the disease of our sin. It is there that healing is found. The blood of Jesus is the atonement that we desperately need. The book of Leviticus reminds us that apart from God, we are all unclean in the sight of God, but in Him, we are made clean and righteous. Healing is found in Jesus.

"Jesus is the answer to the problem of sin that is in all of us."

How does reading chapter 13 expand your understanding of New Testament passages referring to lepers as marginalized in society? See Matthew 8:2-3.

How does this picture of the uncleanliness of disease add to your understanding of the decay that entered the world when the fall occurred?

Re-read Leviticus 15:31. What can we learn about God's holiness from this verse? What can we learn about His graciousness?

Leviticus 16-18

The Day of Atonement is an important and significant event for the people of Israel, but its meaning is so much deeper than we might first think.

Every detail points to Jesus and the redemption that He brings. During the Day of Atonement, we see two goats presented; one is to be a sin offering, and one is to be the scapegoat. The goat for the sin offering is sacrificed to cover the people's sin. The scapegoat is used to symbolize the removal of the people's sins. They are both a picture of Jesus. He is the perfect sacrifice for our sin. His blood is the substitutionary atonement that frees us from the penalty of death that sin threatens to bring upon us, and He is also the one who bears our sin and carries it far away. The priests would confess the sins of the people over the second goat. The goat would bear the weight and penalty of the people's sin and carry it far away. In the same way, Jesus takes the weight and penalty of our sin, and He bore it on the cross. He took the wrath of God in our place so that we could be set free. And now God has carried our sin as far as the east is from the west (Psalm 103:12). The yearly Day of Atonement pointed to a greater day when Jesus would be our atoning sacrifice and carry our sin far away.

The symbolism continues as the priests cleanse themselves. This reminds us that Jesus is the one who cleanses our sin, and He needs no cleansing to enter into the holy place (Hebrews 7:26-28). The pure white garments that priests wear also point us to Jesus and remind us of the perfection and purity of Jesus, who is our great and holy High Priest. He is the one who entered the holy place once for all, not based on the blood of goats and calves but because He has shed His blood for our redemption (Hebrews 9:12). We are made clean because of who He is and what He has done for us.

Every verse on every page points to Him. Even in the midst of bloody sacrifices, pure white garments, and goats running into the wilderness, one theme emerges—the theme of redemption wrapped in the person of Jesus. Even the book of Leviticus should compel us to worship God for who He is and all that He has done.

"We are made clean because of who He is and what He has done for us."

Think for a while longer about the roles the two goats have in the Day of Atonement. Write down the ways that each goat represents what was accomplished by Jesus Christ.

Leviticus 17:7-8 uses powerful language to describe what our hearts do when they wander from the fold of God. Reflect for a moment on how your heart can tend to be unfaithful and how that may reflect your walk with God.

In Leviticus 18:1-5, two things are repeated—the declaration from God of who He is and the command to keep His statutes and ordinances and no one else's. How might this be significant?

Leviticus 19-21

He is holy, and He has commanded His people to be holy as He is holy. This passage finds us looking at the command of holiness in our dealings with other people, personal morality, and the worship of God. In this section, we see highlighted commands for loving our neighbors and those of other nations, sexual purity, fleeing from fortune-telling, and a call for justice. We also see stern warnings regarding the consequences of sin and the devastation of idolatry. God wanted to sanctify and purify His people for Himself. Leviticus 20:26 reminds us that He called His people to be holy and that God had delivered the people for Himself.

The command to holiness can seem overwhelming to us, and we may even feel like we are sinking under the weight of this expectation—but there is hope. The Old Testament law was not given to show us how to achieve perfection, but instead, it was given to point out our need for a Savior. The standard is impossible for us on our own, but Jesus has already made a way for us. Jesus came because we could not fulfill the law in our own strength. In His sinless and perfect life, He has fulfilled every part of the law.

Every verse from Genesis to Revelation is pointing to Jesus and the grand story of redemption (John 5:39, 46). In Matthew, Jesus said that He did not come to abolish the law but to fulfill it (Matthew 5:17-18). Every piece of the story points to Jesus. Jesus has changed everything for us. He has paid the price and made a way to God. And now, when God looks at us, He sees the righteousness of Jesus. Holiness is found in the Holy One.

"Every verse from Genesis to Revelation is pointing to Jesus and the grand story of redemption."

Chapter 19 is largely about how we interact with those around us in a holy manner. Reflect for a moment on how you may not measure up to some of these commands, and then think about how that enables you to reflect and truly understand God's holiness and Christ's gracious sacrifice.

At the beginning of chapter 20, we see God's abhorrence for those who worship Molech. After reading so much about God's holiness, why do you think that the worship of Molech was such a great offense? See Leviticus 20:3.

After reading chapter 21 and seeing the strict guidelines for priests, we understand that earthly priests had to continually follow the rules and practices to be ceremonially clean. With this knowledge, how does your understanding of Christ as the Great High Priest grow?

Leviticus 22-24

In chapters 22-24, we look at the feasts of Israel.

The purpose of the feasts is to point the people's hearts to the Lord so that they will remember who He is and what He has done. The Old Testament feasts are very important to the people as they help them remember God's deliverance and stir their hearts for God. But each feast also points to Jesus and the unfolding story of redemption.

The Passover reminds God's people of Egypt and points to Jesus, who is our Passover Lamb. Jesus is the one who causes God's wrath to pass over those who have put their faith in His saving grace. The first and best was brought in the Feast of Firstfruits, but it also foreshadowed Jesus, who was the first and best God gave for our salvation. At the Feast of Weeks, God's provision was celebrated. And now we know that Jesus is the true provision that God has provided for sinful man to be redeemed. The Feast of Trumpets is a call out of apathy and a reminder of God's covenant love. For believers today, the Lord's Supper reminds us to examine ourselves and remember what Jesus has done for us. In the Day of Atonement, we remember that Jesus is our atonement and the answer to our sin. Our sin is covered and washed clean by His sacrificial and substitutionary atonement. The Feast of Booths looks back to when God delivered His people from Egypt and looks forward to the day when Jesus would dwell with them (John 1:14).

The book of Leviticus preaches the gospel to us. It declares that we are sinful and broken and that we desperately need a Savior. We need atonement. We need a perfect sacrifice. Jesus is who we need. He is foreshadowed and proclaimed in the feasts and in the tabernacle. Every page of God's Word points us to Him as the only answer for our need. We can read Leviticus and rejoice because God has kept His covenant promises. He has done what He said He would do, and now we can trust Him for every moment of every day.

"Jesus is who we need."

QUESTIONS

Reread Leviticus 22:32-33. Once again, we hear God declaring who He is, what Israel must do, who Israel is, and what He has done for them. How can we benefit from dwelling on these declarations? See Philippians 4:8.

As you read about the Old Testament feasts, think about modern seasons that we celebrate, such as Lent or Advent. How can we learn to routinely remember what God has done and praise Him for such from the practice of these feasts?

Once again, think about the holiness that God requires of us. What can we learn about God from His intolerance for blasphemy?

Leviticus 25-27

The story of Scripture is about redemption and restoration.

These traits are so ingrained in God's character that we see them in Scripture over and over again. The beginning of the Old Testament shows the destruction and devastation of sin. However, Leviticus 25 offers rest and restoration from the effects of sin in the Sabbath years and Jubilee. This showcases God's heart for freedom and His plan for redemption. It is a picture of Jesus, who one day brings complete freedom.

The Year of Jubilee would occur every fifty years. It was a year that debts were forgiven, captives were set free, property was restored, and joy returned to the people. For many, this year brought sweet relief from the burdens that they carried. But the Year of Jubilee was only pointing to the One who gives true freedom. It points to Jesus, who would break the chains of sin and destroy our yoke of bondage. We can search this entire world for satisfaction, but true freedom and joy are found only in Jesus (Galatians 5:1, 2 Corinthians 3:17). Isaiah later speaks words of prophecy about the Year of Jubilee (Isaiah 61), and Jesus will read those words in the temple and proclaim that He was the fulfillment (Luke 4:16-30). In Christ, the prisoners are set free. In Him, good news is brought to the poor. In Him, all is restored, and we experience God's favor. We experience a spiritual Jubilee now, and someday we will experience the fullness of this promise as we dwell forever with our God.

The rest of the book of Leviticus reminds us of the covenant. Moses describes the blessings that come for obedience and the consequences of disobedience. God was faithfully working to bring about His promises. He confirmed His covenant with His people and declared over and over that He is the Lord. The truth is valuable for us because it is in knowing who God is that all of the other things of this life are put into perspective. He is the faithful one, and we give our lives to Him.

"He is the faithful one, and we give our lives to Him."

Think about the freedom ancient Israel must have felt during the Year of Jubilee. Do we, as believers who are a part of a new covenant in Christ, continually experience renewed joy in the freedom we experience in Christ?

In Leviticus 26:9, we see God confirming His covenant that He made in Genesis with Abraham, and we see that God does not forget His promises. How can we be comforted by this?

We see God repeating the declaration that He is Lord. Now that we have finished reading the book of Leviticus, why do you think this is significant?

abounding
in faithful
love

Numbers

GENRE: Law, Historical Narrative

AUTHOR / DATE WRITTEN

Moses • c. 1440-1400 BC

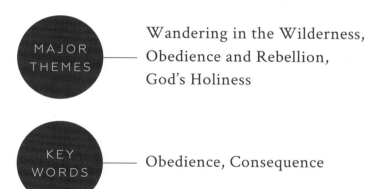

MAJOR THEMES — Wandering in the Wilderness, Obedience and Rebellion, God's Holiness

KEY WORDS — Obedience, Consequence

KEY VERSE

NUMBERS 14:18

The Lord is slow to anger and abounding in faithful love, forgiving iniquity and rebellion. But he will not leave the guilty unpunished, bringing the consequences of the fathers' iniquity on the children to the third and fourth generation.

Numbers 1-3

We have now come to the book of Numbers. Numbers is the fourth book in our journey through Scripture to view the grand story of redemption.

Like Leviticus, Numbers is a book that is often passed over, but amid genealogies, we will see the story of a people who have been freed from the bondage of Egypt and now seek to serve God in the wilderness. We see the formation of a nation and all that will take place in their journey to the Promised Land. There will be many times that they will praise the Lord and rejoice, and there will be many times that they will fail. And every step of the way, He will be faithful. So the book begins with a call for a census. And though these lists of genealogies are not always our favorite things to read, we must remember that these were real people who were leaving the past behind to follow after God. This is the story of God's covenant love and faithfulness to His covenant people.

Their story is not that much different than our own. We have also been freed from bondage. And, we now serve the Lord in the wilderness of this life. We will serve Him, we will praise Him, and we will fail Him. There will be times we forget to trust Him and times this world will entice us. Yet through it all, His steadfast love remains. Though we have failed, He never does. He is faithful, even when we are not.

Numbers begins with a census. The lists of names may feel foreign or disconnected from us. But this list of names is the record of the family of our Messiah, Jesus Christ. And if we are His people, this is our family as well. The history of the people of Israel is our history because we have been grafted into a spiritual family far greater than a national family. This story is our story because this is the story to which every verse points. This is the story of our redemption.

"This story is our story because this is the story to which every verse points."

Reflect on the ways that you can relate to Israel—how you might experience seasons of great faithfulness to God and periods of rebellion as well. How does this grow your understanding of God's steadfastness to His people?

The entire first chapter details the census taken by Moses. This census will later help track the genealogy of Jesus Christ millennia later. What does this tell us about the purposes of God, regardless of time passed?

In chapter 3, we are reminded of Nadab and Abihu's disobedience to the Lord. Because this is the second time that it is mentioned, what can we learn about the impact of our sin?

Numbers 4-6

As we dig more deeply into the book of Numbers, we begin seeing the different tribes and people groups of the nation of Israel.

Each group is listed as well as the specific duties and calling of each group. God had given each group a distinct role to fulfill. In the same way, each one of us has specific gifts and callings. They are all different, but each one is important and necessary for the body of Christ to function as it should. The work that He has called you to do is meaningful, and He has uniquely equipped you to do it. Do not let your heart get distracted or discouraged by what He has called others to do. Put everything you have into the calling He has given you. After all, the church is made up of many people with many different gifts and callings who were specifically equipped to serve (1 Corinthians 12:12, Romans 12:4). God created us to serve Him uniquely and corporately.

This passage continues to remind us of the uncleanness of our sin and the need for confession. Our hearts are pointed to Jesus, who is the only one with the power and authority to make us clean. When we confess, we can be sure that He will forgive us.

The section wraps up in chapter 6 with the blessing given by God for Aaron to give to all people. There are many tribes with many different duties, but they are all God's chosen and covenant people. Our identity is not found in who we are but in whose we are. The words of this blessing are beautiful and poetic, and Jesus fulfills them. He is the one who blesses us and keeps us. He is the one who has shined His light on us. He is the one who has extended grace. He is the one who brings us peace.

"Our hearts are pointed to Jesus, who is the only one with the power and authority to make us clean."

QUESTIONS

In chapter 4, we begin to learn the different duties of specific clans within Israel. How does this correlate to the way God designed His church to operate?

Reread Numbers 5:1-4. Reflect on how what is designated unclean will contaminate all who touch it. What does this tell us about the need to keep ourselves holy by ridding ourselves of sin through the power of Christ?

Spend time reflecting on Aaron's blessing in Numbers 6:22-27. Think about the diversity that exists within the church. How can you take comfort in this blessing, knowing that this was given freely to the Israelites, regardless of their giftings?

Numbers 7-9

Numbers 7-9 describes the offerings and instructions for the tabernacle.

The tabernacle is where God dwells with the people, so these instructions are vital. The sacrifices and cleansing of the priests foreshadow a far greater spiritual reality. The sacrifices designed to make atonement for people's sins remind us of the weight of our sin and point us to Jesus, who is the only one who can be a once and for all sacrifice for the sins of His people. It is also here that we see God speak to Moses from the mercy seat. With the tabernacle in place, there was now a central location through which God could dwell with His people.

In chapter 9, the nation celebrates Passover. This is the most important feast for the people. It reminds them of how God delivered them from Egypt, and it is a picture of the salvation that would come through Jesus. The blood of the true, spotless Lamb spares us from death. Remembering what God has done in the past increases our faith and helps us trust God for the future. As the children of Israel looked back to Passover, we can look back to the cross where our Passover Lamb took our sin away (John 1:29). Remembering reminds us of who God is and what He has done for us and in our place.

At the end of the chapter, we see how the people were led by the cloud and fire of God's presence. God's Spirit now leads us in the same way (Romans 8:14). Let us be people who are sensitive to His voice and ready to answer His call. Even in the wilderness, we are led by our God. The people waited for the leading of God before they ever picked up camp. May the same be true of us.

Reread Numbers 7:89. Think about how comforting yet awe-inspiring it must have been to finally have a meeting place with God. How does this grow your understanding of affection for receiving the Holy Spirit when we become Christians?

As you read about the consecration of the Levites in chapter 8, think about all that God required from them so that they would be exclusively assigned to God (v. 16). How does this expand your understanding of Jesus Christ being the ultimate Great High Priest?

Think about the discipline required of the Israelites to truly wait on the command of the Lord for whether to travel. Reread Numbers 9:22. Are you willing to wait on the Lord's command in this manner?

Numbers 10-12

What is the one thing in life that you desire and do not have? We all have things we want, and the children of Israel were no different.

Chapter 10 opens as the people set out from Sinai (they had been there since Exodus 19), and it seems like they make a good start. They leave Sinai, following God's presence, and we are hopeful that they will follow the Lord to the Promised Land. But it does not take long for them to begin complaining. The first complaint comes because they do not have meat to eat. They glamorize their past slavery and complain about where God has them.

God was working miracles each day as He rained down manna from heaven and led them with the pillars of cloud and fire, but they were not satisfied. The manna was the bread from heaven, and the descriptions tell us that it must have tasted heavenly as well, but the people were still not satisfied. They missed all that God had done for them because they were consumed by the one thing He had not done. How often we find ourselves in the same situation and with the same struggle as the children of Israel. Let us not miss all that God has done for us because of the one thing we desire and do not have. Let us trust that He is good and that His way is perfect (Psalm 18:30). He has provided everything that we need, even when we do not understand why there are things that we do not have.

The bread from heaven points us to Jesus, the true manna, the true bread from heaven (John 6:31-35). He has been given for our salvation. He is all that we need. Yet, we often turn to worthless idols thinking that some satisfaction can be found in them. But peace and satisfaction for our souls can only be found in Jesus. He is the only bread that satisfies.

"The bread from heaven points us to Jesus, the true manna, the true bread from heaven."

QUESTIONS

Take a moment to examine your life. Are there things that the Lord has provided for you, as He did manna for the Israelites, that have grown dull to you? Spend some time in prayer, asking God to renew your joy in His goodness to provide for you, and praise Him for His steadfastness.

Reflect on God's provision of help to Moses in Numbers 11:12-17. In what ways has God provided relief of burdens for you?

In Numbers 12:3, the Lord describes Moses's humility. Spend some time in self-reflection and examination. What would the Lord say about your humility? Do you seek to glorify God more than yourself?

Numbers 13-15

This passage shows God ready to fulfill a promise that He has made and the people's lack of faith.

God promised the people the land of Canaan. It was a done deal in God's eyes. So, Moses sent twelve spies in to look at the land. They were not supposed to be deciding whether to take the land, but instead, they were to make a plan for how they would do it. God intended this trip as a way for them to get a glimpse of what God had in store for them in this land.

Joshua and Caleb have faith in what God would do, but the other ten spies see too many obstacles. In the end, the people listen to the ten complaining spies, and God says that the people would have to wait. The people refused to trust God and claim the promise that He had already made to His people. All they had to do was walk into the land that God had promised and set before them, but instead, this generation would die in the wilderness, and it would be their children who would enter the Promised Land.

In this passage, we see a sinful people and a righteous God. And we see Moses standing between as an intercessor for the people. Moses was an imperfect picture of Jesus, who is our intercessor. He is the one who intercedes in our weakness and covers us in His perfect righteousness.

It is easy to shake our heads at the Israelites and wonder how they did not trust the Lord after everything that He had done for them. He delivered them from Egypt. He led them in the wilderness. He gave them food to eat and water to drink. He provided for them every step of the way. However, we must also remember the times we have done the same thing. We struggle to trust the Lord to do what He has said He will do. We forget to remember all of the ways that He has proven His faithfulness to us. Let us trust Him no matter what. He is good, and He is trustworthy. We can rest in His plan.

"He is good, and He is trustworthy."

In what ways can you relate to the spies sent to Canaan? Do you struggle with trusting God's plan when His plan seems impossible by earthly standards?

Reflect on the power of words, as shown by the spies' attempt to thwart God's plan. What does this teach you about the power of your tongue and the necessity that you speak the truth?

Reread Numbers 15:37-41 with the acknowledgment that they did not have access to Scripture in the same way that modern Christians do. How does this add to your understanding of the importance of dwelling on the Word of God? What are some practical steps you can take to remind yourself of His Word on a regular basis?

Numbers 16-18

Numbers 16 records the shocking account of Korah's rebellion.

Korah gathered a group from the people of Israel to rebel against Moses and His leadership. Since Moses had been put into authority by God, this was actually a rebellion against God. In Numbers 16:13-14, the people even used the language of milk and honey that described the Promised Land to describe Egypt where they were in slavery. They glamorized their time of bondage and blamed Moses for not taking them into the true Promised Land. They ignored that it was their sin that caused them not to enter the land. As a consequence of their rebellion, God caused the earth to swallow them up.

The time in the wilderness is marked by complaining and rebelling from the people. But it is also marked by the constant, steadfast love and faithfulness of God to His people. Over and over again, they would fail, and time and time again, He would prove His love and faithfulness. The people certainly do not deserve the mercy and love extended to them.

However, God's faithfulness was never based on their, or our, ability to earn God's love. God's steadfast love and faithfulness are always based on who He is. God is holy, just, faithful, and merciful. Though the children of Israel failed to see His provision and deliverance, He never changed. And after all of their rebellion and complaining, God gave them the priesthood, which points them to Jesus, who would be the final Great High priest.

How often have we failed the Lord and complained despite all that He has done for us? And yet His steadfast love and mercy remain. We will fail Him, but He will never fail us.

"God's steadfast love and faithfulness are always based on who He is."

100

QUESTIONS

Reflect on the whole of chapter 16. List the characteristics of God that you see represented throughout the narrative, and dwell on how they all work in tandem.

Aaron's staff served as a reminder of God's choice. What are some reminders that God uses in your life to point you toward Him?

In Numbers 18, God provides for those who serve Him. How does this encourage you to rest in His ability to provide for you as you serve Him?

Numbers 19-21

The laws for purity continue to set forth a reminder of our uncleanness due to sin and our need for the cleansing that can only come through Christ.

Chapter 20 brings to us the death of Miriam and a pivotal moment in the book when God commands Moses to speak to the rock so that it will bring forth water. Instead of obeying the command of God, Moses strikes the rock. God provides water for the people that day. But He also tells Moses that because of His disobedience, He would not be able to enter into the Promised Land. The heaviness of that realization is difficult for us, but it should serve as a reminder of the weight and consequences of our sin. Aaron would die in the wilderness as well, and the people would weep over the loss, but God would continue to be faithful to His unfaithful people. He would lead them in battle, defeat their enemies, and provide a song in the wilderness for them.

Look and live. This message rings out for us in chapter 21. The nation of Israel had just won a great military victory, and though they should have been praising and rejoicing, they are complaining again. God had given them victory in the battle and had provided for them, but they grew impatient that the situation is not what they expected it to be. So the Lord sends poisonous snakes, and soon the people are confessing their sins. In Numbers 21:8-9, God gives Moses some peculiar instructions—to lift up a bronze serpent on a pole so that those who have been bitten could look and live.

We have no question about the meaning of this event as Jesus tells us in John 3:14-15. Just as the serpent was lifted up in the wilderness, Jesus would be lifted up to draw all men to Himself and give everyone an opportunity to look and live (John 12:32). And just like the serpent in the wilderness, our healing and salvation come when we look to God in faith and live. Even in our rebellion and complaining, He made a way of redemption. Look to Him and live.

Continue to think about the phrase, "Look to Him and live." What does this encourage you to do as you grow in your walk with God?

In Numbers 20:12, the Lord chastens Moses and Aaron for not trusting Him to demonstrate His holiness to the Israelites and striking the rock instead of speaking to it as God had commanded. What does this say about what we accomplish in our wisdom versus what God accomplishes when we obey His wisdom?

Reread Numbers 21:22-25. What can we learn about God from these verses? Do you truly believe that He will accomplish what He has called you to do in obedience?

Numbers 22-24

In these chapters, we are introduced to Balaam, the reluctant prophet.

Balak hires Balaam to curse Israel, but it will not come to pass because it is not part of God's plan. Balaam is stopped in his tracks quite literally when his donkey speaks to him, and the angel of the Lord appears. Balaam prophesied four times, and despite Balak's request for cursing, his prophecies are full of blessing for the nation of Israel. In fact, he even prophesied of the Messiah who was to come in Numbers 24:17. A speaking donkey was certainly not a normal occurrence, but God has the power to use anything to bring about His will. God used a speaking donkey, and God used Balaam despite his unwillingness. God is sovereign over all things, and He has the power to bend anything to His ways. The account of Balaam reminds us of God's power and our weakness. Yet, even through the weakness of man, God shows His strength.

These chapters are a testament to God's faithful and steadfast love for His people. Though they often complained, God had chosen them and set them apart for a special purpose, and He brings His purposes to pass. We can be assured of the same truth—that God is on our side if we are His children, and nothing will thwart His plans. We can be confident in the truth found in Romans 8:31, which says if God is for us, no one can be against us. We can rest in His plan. The account of Balaam is a testament of God's sovereignty, steadfast love, and protection for His people.

Balaam pronounced blessing on God's people, and the ultimate fulfillment of that blessing would come through the blessed One who would be born out of the line of Abraham. The scepter that would rise was none other than Jesus our Messiah. And God proclaimed all this through a donkey and an unlikely prophet.

"We can rest in His plan."

QUESTIONS

God uses a donkey to thwart human plans that were against His plans. What unconventional things might God be using in your life to get your attention and turn your ways back to His ways?

Take a moment to think about Numbers 23:12 when Balaam says, "Shouldn't I say exactly what the Lord puts in my mouth?" As modern Christians, the Lord puts the whole of Scripture in our mouths; the Bible is readily available for us to immerse ourselves in. Is your mouth a source of truth, proclaiming the greatness of God and the good news of the gospel to those around you?

In Numbers 24:12-14, Balaam denounces earthly rewards for the sake of obedience to the Lord. How does this expand your understanding of the rewards this world has for us versus the heavenly reward we have in God?

Numbers 25-27

God is serious about holiness. That is made clear in these chapters as we see the impact of sin on the people.

It is here that we see the census of the second generation. The first generation was delivered from the bondage of Egypt. Yet, they failed to trust the Lord when He wanted to deliver them into the Promised Land, and the consequence of that sin was that they would not enter into the land. Instead, God said that the next generation would be the ones to enter. In this passage, we see the census of the generation that would go in.

The time to enter the long-awaited Promised Land was finally getting closer. God made it clear that Moses would see the land of Canaan, but because of his sin, he would not be able to enter. A new leader would need to be chosen. The nation would need a strong and faithful man to lead them as Moses had faithfully done for many years.

The nation of Israel was full of people who rebelled and questioned the Lord, but God would need just one faithful man. That man is Joshua. He is a man who has been faithful and stood for what was right even when it was not the popular thing to do. Joshua is rewarded for his faithfulness to the Lord. We also should seek to follow the Lord, even when it is not what everyone is doing. In a sea of complainers and those who question the Lord, let us be people who trust Him and follow Him no matter what.

Moses and Joshua were great leaders and deliverers of the people. Yet they simply served to point to the One, Jesus, who would be our greatest leader and deliverer. Every step of the story leads us to the day when the true deliverer will come. When He comes, He will pay the price for the sin once and for all and rescue His people from the bondage of sin.

"Let us be people who trust Him and follow Him no matter what."

Reflect on the things that God has given you, both material and eternal. What are some of the ways you can give to God out of a gracious heart in thanksgiving for all that He has done?

In Numbers 13, we discover that 10 of the spies did not trust God and two did. Yet, only Joshua is appointed to take Moses's place as Israel's leader out of the two faithful spies. What does this tell you about the consequences of obeying God?

Read Colossians 1:12-14 and Psalm 103:1-5. Spend some time in prayerful thanksgiving to the Lord for all that He has done for us.

Numbers 28-30

In Numbers 28-30, we are again reminded of the detailed sacrificial system.

The sacrifices and offerings are a huge part of the lives of the Israelite people. There are daily offerings, weekly offerings, monthly offerings, and those that occur once a year during a specific feast. The Hebrews' lives are marked with the perpetual reminder of their sin and their desperate need for atonement.

But these sacrifices and this law were just a shadow of what was to come, as the author of Hebrews tells us in Hebrews 10:1. The people spent their days, weeks, months, and years making sacrifices, but Jesus would come and change everything. Jesus would be the once for all sacrifice. He is the spotless Lamb who takes away the sins of the world (Hebrews 10:12-14, Romans 6:10). The Israelites offered their sacrifices as a way of acknowledging their sin and looking forward to the One who would be the final atonement. And now we can look back to the cross where Jesus, the spotless Lamb, covered our sins.

Romans 12:1-2 also gives us great insight into what life should look like for the Christian who has experienced redemption because of Jesus's sacrifice on the cross. Our response to the sacrifice of Jesus should be to offer up our bodies as a worshipful sacrifice. The gospel cannot be earned, but it should compel us to act out of a heart of overflowing gratitude for all that God has done for us.

Chapter 30 also gives us a glimpse at the importance of vows to the Lord. Our God is a God of faithfulness, and He wants us to reflect His character in this way. We are called to be faithful as He is faithful. This faithfulness is not possible in our own strength, and that is why the reading of the law must always point us to the cross where Jesus demonstrated His love for His people. He is always faithful. He always keeps His covenant promises.

"We are called to be faithful as He is faithful."

As you read and think about the offering required of the Israelites, reflect on what God requires of His people today. List the ways that Jesus has exemplified these sacrifices for us all.

Take a moment to reread the first two verses of chapter 30. How does this command measure up to the faithfulness that we have seen God show through keeping His promises?

In chapter 30, we see the seriousness with which God takes marriage vows. How does this add to your understanding of the church being the bride of Christ?

Numbers 31-33

God is forming the nation of Israel, and while doing so,
He is revealing His plans for them.

The first generation—who had come out of Egypt—died in the wilderness after refusing to trust the Lord to allow them to enter. Now the second generation was getting ready to enter this long-awaited Promised Land. God had great and beautiful land for them, but they often wanted to do things their way. God has set aside the beautiful Promised Land for them, but they still want to settle for land that is less than God's best for them. In chapter 32, we see that the people ask God to give them a lesser land. It seemed so much easier in the moment, but it was far from God's best for them. They were struggling to trust that God would do what He had promised He would do. We often do the same. We are willing to take the easier road that will give us something good instead of waiting for God's perfect plan. We struggle to trust in His faithfulness though He has never once failed us.

Almost all of the Israelites fall into this trap, but there are two, Joshua and Caleb, who are wholly dedicated to the Lord, and it is recorded here. What a precious reminder that God sees our quiet faithfulness, even when it seems like no one else does. But even more than that, we can see these faithful men who led their people, pointing us to the true and better faithful leader we find in Jesus. He is the one who will lead us safely home.

In chapter 33, all of the places the Israelites traveled on their wilderness journey are recorded. God knew and saw every place they were, but most of all, He went with them every step of the way. Child of God, if you feel like you are all alone, take comfort in this truth: He knows every step that you take, and He has never left your side. He is with you. Even in the wilderness, His grace is ever-present.

"God sees our quiet faithfulness, even when it seems like no one else does."

What are some of the ways you may be settling in contentedness for things that are less than God's perfect plan?

In Numbers 31:21-24, we see imagery regarding fire and water as purifying agents. How does this grow your understanding of Matthew 3:11?

In Numbers 33:50-56, we see specific instructions that the Lord has for entering the Promised Land. Reflect on the ways that you have grown in your understanding of the Lord's commands from reading through the book of Numbers.

Numbers 34-36

In these chapters, the nation of Israel receives more instruction regarding all of the details of the Promised Land they would inherit.

They are given all of the specifics about their inheritance. They are told the borders and boundary lines, how the Levites would be divided, and they are given instruction on the cities of refuge and what happens to one's inheritance.

While the account we have been reading tells us about the inheritance of the Promised Land, Scripture also tells us that there is a greater inheritance to come for those who trust in the Messiah. The New Testament is clear that we are heirs to a heavenly inheritance (Romans 8:17, Galatians 3:29). The Old Testament Scripture is pointing to a future fulfillment. And while the Promised Land may have been reserved for the nation of Israel, there is an inheritance that is coming for every follower of Jesus. As we sense the excitement of the Israelites, we are reminded that we, too, are waiting for the day we will enter the Promised Land He has prepared for us.

The book of Numbers points us to the steadfast love and holiness of God. It also reminds us of our weakness and stumbling faith, just like the people wandering in the wilderness and the faithful God who always brings about His sovereign purpose. The last words of Chapter 35 remind us of a God who longs to dwell with His people, and John 1:14 reminds us that God came, in the form of Jesus, to this earth and dwelt among us to redeem His people. God with us, our Immanuel, came to dwell among sinful people and lived a perfect life that fulfilled every part of the law on behalf of sinful people who could never measure up. So the book of Numbers should cause us to rejoice because we do not have to strive to fulfill this law on our own. We can rest in the One who has fulfilled it for us, and we can pursue a life of holiness only because of His Spirit within us.

"We can pursue a life of holiness only because of His Spirit within us."

QUESTIONS

As you reflect on Promised Land coming to fruition for the Israelites, also think about what our inheritance is now as Christians. Use Romans 8:17, Galatians 3:29, and 1 Peter 1:3-4 to develop your understanding of our inheritance.

Reread the final verse of chapter 35, where we are once again reminded of the holiness of God. How does this verse expand your understanding of holiness, as our bodies are now the dwelling place of the Holy Spirit?

Now that we have finished reading the book of Numbers, spend some time dwelling on the things you have learned about God, His holiness, and His demand for us to be consecrated. Below, paraphrase some of the things you have learned.

Love the Lord Your God.

Deuteronomy

GENRE: Law, Historical Narrative

AUTHOR / DATE WRITTEN
Moses • c. 1406 BC

 MAJOR THEMES —— Obedience, Faithfulness, Remembering the Lord

 KEY WORDS —— Law, Obey, Remember

KEY VERSES

DEUTERONOMY 6:4-6

Listen, Israel: The Lord our God, the Lord is one. Love the Lord your God with all your heart, with all your soul, and with all your strength. These words that I am giving you today are to be in your heart.

Deuteronomy 1-3

The book of Deuteronomy opens with Moses retelling all that the Lord had done and where the people have come from after they triumphantly left Egypt.

The Lord was with them every step of the way. Though the people had times of rebellion and complaining, the steadfast love of the Lord was constant and sure. He was faithful to His people. In all of their wanderings in the wilderness, God never left their side. He led them through seas and deserts and fought battles in their name. God had given them exactly what they needed every step of the way. He was fulfilling His covenant promises that He made to Abraham. And the Lord led them through every moment.

Moses recounts how the first generation refused to enter into the Promised Land that God prepared for them. They rebelled and refused to trust His almighty hand. They were skeptical about whether or not God would keep His promises, and ultimately, they decided to trust in human wisdom. They trusted in their strength instead of resting in the Lord's. They decided that they did not want to go in. They lacked the faith required to live in the Promised Land. So the first generation would never enter the land. Instead, it would be a new generation. The book of Deuteronomy will be a retelling of the law to a new generation.

We would do well to spend time remembering God's faithfulness to us. Our faith is renewed when we look back at the markers of His grace and faithfulness to us. We are encouraged when we are reminded that He is fighting for us, and we are comforted when we are confident that He is always with us. We lack nothing because of Him. The people of Israel were needy people who had failed to be faithful. But their faithlessness only served to point to the faithful One. God would keep every promise, including the promise to send Jesus, the Redeemer, because the promises of God are dependent on Him and not on us.

"We would do well to spend time remembering God's faithfulness to us."

What are some ways God continues to be faithful to you and provide for you?

In Deuteronomy 1:8, we are again reminded of the covenant God made with Abraham. How does this reminder encourage you to hold fast to God's steadfast faithfulness to keep His promises?

Reread Deuteronomy 3:22. How can you take comfort in the promise that God will be victorious for us?

Deuteronomy 4-6

As Moses recounts the journey that the nation of Israel has been on since Egypt, he pays special attention to the character of God.

At each step along their long journey, the people were learning more and more about who God is and how who He is changes everything. Our God is great, and Moses tells of some of the ways that His greatness is displayed.

He is near. Whenever we call, He is there (Deuteronomy 4:7). What a comfort to us to know that He is always there. He is a God who keeps His covenants (Deuteronomy 4:29-31). Everything He has promised, He will do. There is no one like our God (Deuteronomy 4:35). He is the only God, and there is no one like Him. Who He is should dictate how we live. His love for us and our love for Him should compel us to be consumed with His Word because it is in His Word that we learn who He is. Scripture is how we come to know Him more. When we truly get a glimpse of who God is, our hearts will yearn to know Him more. We must linger in His Word and allow His Word to become part of us and our day-to-day lives.

These chapters are full of the beautiful character of God and the blessings that come from obedience, but they are also full of warnings of the consequences of disobedience. Within these chapters, we see the Ten Commandments recounted for the people, and great emphasis is given to warnings about idolatry. Deuteronomy 6:4-9 contains the famous Shema that was a very important passage for the people of Israel. It declared that there is one God and that the people were to love Him above all and teach this truth to their children. God's Word was to be always on their hearts, minds, and lips. God was about to give the people good things that they could not earn, and He wanted them to remember who He is. In Jesus, we are given what we could never earn on our own. Just as the people would receive a land of promise, we receive an inheritance from God. We could not earn it, but it has been given as a gift of grace.

Continue to think about the importance of lingering in God's Word. What are some things that might be stopping you from doing this daily? List them below, and ask the Lord to give you the strength to dwell on Him daily.

In chapter 5, before Moses reads the Ten Commandments, there is another declaration of who God is and what He has done. How does continually remembering who God is and what He has done encourage you toward obedience?

Spend some time reflecting on Deuteronomy 6:4-9. How does this passage encourage you to store up the treasure of Scripture in your heart?

Deuteronomy 7-9

God's love for His chosen people is indescribable.

He always keeps His covenants, and He never forsakes those who love Him. In this section of Scripture, we are reminded of the importance of remembering the Lord and all He has done. In chapter 7, we are reminded that God will be faithful to the promises that He made to Abraham. He had chosen the Israelites out of all nations, not because they were great but because He is great. He set His love upon them even though they had no merit.

God sometimes allows His children to hunger so that He can fill them. The Lord allows the people to hunger but then provides manna for them to eat. Sometimes the Lord must remind us of our great need for Him so that we will run to Him instead of trying to live in our strength. Later, He reminds the people not to forget Him during times of prosperity. We often run to the Lord in times of need and then try to do things in our strength when life is easy. We must be careful not to allow pride to creep into our hearts. We must constantly remind ourselves that all success comes from the Lord. It is not by our strength but by His power (Deuteronomy 8:17-18). The Lord will never forsake His children, and we must constantly be preaching to our hearts and reminding ourselves to seek Him in all things.

The choosing of Israel is an illustration of the election of God's people. He chooses His own from every tribe, tongue, and nation. He does not choose them because of any good inside them, but He chooses them in grace and mercy. The cross demonstrates the overwhelming and indescribable love of God for the people He sought to redeem. He has pursued His own.

"We must constantly be preaching to our hearts and reminding ourselves to seek Him in all things."

Deuteronomy 7:9 reminds us that God's faithfulness exists not because we deserve it but because He is good. What are some of the ways that God has remained faithful to you despite you not deserving it?

Again, in Deuteronomy 8:17-18, we are reminded that provision is from the Lord and not from our own strength. How does this grow and expand your understanding of the circumstances God allows in your life?

Chapter 9 begins with a reminder that the possession of the Promised Land is not because of Israel's greatness but because of the Lord's greatness (v. 4). How can this humble you before the Lord in your day-to-day life?

Deuteronomy 10-12

What does God expect and desire from us? How do we please the Lord?

We often look at the law as a list of rules and requirements, but it really just points out God's holiness and our undeniable need for Him. There are many laws, but the most important thing is that we love the Lord. In Matthew 22:34-40, a pharisee questions Jesus about the most important law, and He points the people back to loving the Lord and tells them that the second is loving our neighbor. The whole law can be summed up in these two commandments. When we love the Lord with everything we are, our service and obedience to Him flow out of that. We do not love Him because we serve Him, but rather, we serve Him because we love Him.

The law does not seem like a burden when we serve from a place of love and dedication to the Lord. It also helps to remember that Jesus kept the law perfectly to cover our failings. Our love for Him compels us to do what is right and praise Him with our lives. Chapter 11 gives the command to lay up these words in our hearts and center our entire lives around the Lord. In God's Word, we learn who He is, and it is in knowing who He is that we love Him. In loving Him with all that we are, we can do what He has called us to do.

Chapter 12 details the instructions for the people to destroy the places where idols are worshiped and worship the Lord in the way that He has instructed the people to do. We cannot keep the law in our own strength, but Jesus has perfectly kept the law in our place. Through His sinless life, He kept every part of the law, and through His death on the cross, He became our perfect sacrifice. Through His resurrection and ascension, He proved that He has power over death and sin. We can delight in the law of God because Jesus has kept it in our place. He has kept it, and He has fulfilled it. Now we rejoice in His finished work and wear the robes of His righteousness (Isaiah 61:10).

"We can delight in the law of God because Jesus has kept it in our place."

Do you find yourself serving God out of the overflow of love you have for Him, or does your love for Him feel based on merit? Spend time in prayer, asking God to help you love Him rightly.

In Deuteronomy 10:12, we see that keeping the Lord's commands is for our own benefit. From your understanding of the testimony of the Israelites, how can you confirm that this is true?

Much of what we have read in Deuteronomy has been about remembering the work of the Lord, and chapter 11 is no different. Having read so much about the journey of Israel into the Promised Land, how is your affection for God stirred by remembering the Lord's work?

Deuteronomy 13-15

As we walk through much of the Law, it is easy to feel like there is not much for us as modern Christians in this ancient Hebrew text.

However, the Law is full of revelation of God's character and principles that can be applied to our daily lives. Though there are cultural commands that do not apply to us, we can often see the heart of God encouraging us to love the Lord and our neighbors.

Chapter 13 shows that we should exercise wisdom and carefully discern against false teachers who seek to arise among the people of God just like they did in the nation of Israel. Chapter 14 reminds us that God's people are to be holy and set apart in every aspect of their lives. God will not forsake His people. God commands holiness and purity. The people could not achieve that on their own and would need sacrifices to atone for their sin. But those sacrifices point us to the final sacrifice that took place on the hill of Calvary. Jesus is the sacrifice who stood in our place. His shed blood makes us clean before God if we have placed faith in His grace. The response to His goodness is worship.

Chapter 15 serves as a reminder to love and give as the Lord has freely loved and given to us. We are encouraged to remember what the Lord has done for us, and then open wide our hands to those around us. As we see God's character displayed throughout Scripture, we are constantly reminded of who He is and all that He has done for us. The overflow of the grace and mercy that has been extended to us causes us to extend grace and mercy to the needy and poor we encounter. Before God, we are poor and needy, yet God has showered us in a grace that allows us to extend grace.

"God has showered us in a grace that allows us to extend grace."

How does chapter 13 increase your wisdom on the relationships to which you hold tight?

Reread Deuteronomy 14:2, and think about the magnitude of that statement from the Lord. List the ways below that you feel comforted by this verse, and spend some time in thankful prayer for God allowing us access to the gospel.

As you read chapter 15, think about how the canceling of debts and lending to those in need demonstrates the graciousness of God. How does your understanding of God's character grow through this chapter?

Deuteronomy 16-18

This time of remembrance was something that they were to do often. The children of Israel would remember what God had done for them through feasts such as Passover. These feasts served to remind them of what the Lord had done and of who He is. It also reminded them that just as the promises made to Abraham were beginning to be fulfilled, God would be faithful to bring forth the Messiah just as He had promised. Jesus is the spotless Lamb who takes away the sins of the world. The entire Passover meal is filled with symbols pointing to Jesus. In Passover, the Hebrew people could look back at their deliverance from Egypt and look forward to the Messiah, who would be their true deliverer.

Deuteronomy 17 would prove to be an important part of the law in the history of the people of Israel. God was setting up laws and providing the people with everything they needed to serve Him and live in the land He was giving to them. We have already seen in the Pentateuch that time after time, the people would live in unfaithfulness, and this would continue throughout Israel's history. In Deuteronomy 17, God establishes laws and guidelines for how kings were supposed to live and rule, and the rejection of these principles would later prove to be disastrous for the people.

But God would provide. He would be faithful to His unfaithful people. In the immediate future, He would raise up a godly ruler. But in the distant future, He would provide a leader who was God in the flesh. Jesus is a far better prophet and a far better judge than Israel had ever known. He is the perfect leader of His people.

"Jesus is a far better prophet and a far better judge than Israel had ever known."

To ancient Israel, the Passover feast served as a reminder of the promise of the forthcoming Messiah, and to us, it is a reminder of God's faithfulness that He did provide the Messiah. What are some other ways that remembering Passover expands your understanding of all that God has done for us?

In Deuteronomy 17:7, we see the phrase, "You must purge the evil from you." When talking about idolatry, what are some boundaries you can put up for yourself to keep you from falling into fleshly patterns of loving earthly things more than God?

Reread Deuteronomy 18:20-22. How does this convict you to be sure of the truthfulness of your speech?

Deuteronomy 19-21

God's character, as well as His covenant love for His people, is seen again in this passage.

We see His heart for justice when we look at the plan for the cities of refuge, laws for property boundaries, witnesses, and the laws that deal with crimes. Our God cares for the outcast, the marginalized, and the oppressed.

In chapter 20, amid laws about justice, there are laws concerning warfare and an important lesson about God's heart. The Lord reminds the people that when they face an enemy, they should not fear, for God is with them and will fight for them. In comparison to the other nations, the Hebrew people were small. Though they would face much larger armies, God reminds them that He is on their side. He has brought them to this place and delivered them from Egypt, and He is not going to abandon them now. God would fight for them and give them victory. The same is true for you. God has redeemed you and brought you to this place, and He will not abandon you now. He is on your side. He will fight for you. He is with you. Victory is found in Him.

At the very end of Deuteronomy 21, we find the instruction for the immediate burial of a man hung on a tree, and a curse pronounced for one who hangs on a tree. This points us to Jesus, the Messiah, who bore the curse of our sin on the cross in place of His people. Galatians 3:13 references this text as it tells us that Jesus bore our curse and suffered in our place. Tucked in the law that can feel distant from our current situation are reminders of the One this story is all about. The story of the Bible—including the books of the Law—is about God coming to rescue and redeem His people. This is our story. It is a story formed before the creation of the world. It is a story of redemption. It is the story of Jesus.

"This is our story. It is a story formed before the creation of the world."

Continue to reflect on the fact that we do not have to be fearful that God's plan will be thwarted. Below, list out the ways that this is consoling.

Again we see the phrase, "You must purge the evil from you." Throughout these chapters, take a moment to think about why it is important for us to continually be sanctified before the Lord.

Reread Deuteronomy 21:23. How does this point toward Jesus bearing the wrath of God? How does this deepen your understanding of what was accomplished on the cross?

Deuteronomy 22-24

Our God is holy. We are sinful.

We see this theme repeating in the Old Testament as we think about the laws regarding purity. Every law serves to point us to our need for a redeemer with the power to wash us and make us clean. The laws seem heavy and burdensome to us, which points us to our need and imprints on our hearts the hope of the One who was promised to Abraham. We are yearning for the fulfillment of every promise.

Deuteronomy 23 reminds us of the story of Balaam, and though he had been commanded to curse the children of Israel, God would not allow it and, in fact, turns the curse into a blessing. Deuteronomy 23:5 stands out as a verse demonstrating well the love that our God has for us. Because of God's love for His people, He turns the curse into a blessing. This is repeated time and time throughout Scripture, but we so desperately need for it to sink into our hearts. The story of Joseph in Genesis 50:20 is a great example of this truth. Joesph's brothers planned evil against him, but God turned it for good. Romans 8:28 reminds us again that God uses everything for the good of His people. He loves us. He is on our side. We can trust Him even when the situation seems hopeless. He will turn the curse into a blessing because of His great love for us.

Throughout this passage, we see the command to remember all that God had done for His people. They are urged to think about how God rescued and redeemed them from Egypt. And that remembrance would strengthen their faith and encourage them to live in light of who God is. As we look back to what God has done in our lives, our faith grows. As we look to the cross, we are reminded that Jesus has paid the price that these chapters remind us we could never pay. Remembering gives us faith to trust God to be faithful today and tomorrow, just as He was faithful in the past.

"He will turn the curse into a blessing because of His great love for us."

Take a moment to truly reflect on Romans 8:28. What are some of the ways that you have seen God work things together for the nation of Israel? What are some ways you have seen Him work things together for you?

As you read more about instructions for purity, how is your understanding of God's holiness stretched?

In Deuteronomy 24:22, God commands Israel to remember that they were slaves in the land of Egypt, which is why they should care for the resident aliens of their land. How does the fact that we were once orphans but are now adopted into the Father's fold change your perception of serving the lost around you?

Deuteronomy 25-27

God cares for the outcast, the abandoned, and the helpless.

In chapter 25, we learn about the system of levirate marriage where a man would redeem the wife of his brother who passed away. Widows were at the lowest end of the social strata in this period of time and would have been helpless in the male-dominated society. But God made a way for the helpless to be redeemed from their hopeless situation. This picture of the kinsman-redeemer points us to Jesus, who is our true and better kinsman-redeemer, rescuing us from our hopeless state when we had no power to save ourselves.

In chapter 26, we learn that giving and thanksgiving go hand in hand. When we dwell on all that God has done for us, it will prompt both praises and generosity in our lives. In this passage of Scripture, we are reminded of the law of firstfruits and how we are to give back to the Lord because of all that He has given to us. The people are commanded to give their tithe. It was to be the first of their crops. They are not to wait until the end and give the leftovers but the very first of each crop to the Lord.

However, the law of firstfruits was not just about giving; it also focused on acknowledging and giving thanks to God for all that He had done. Giving is an act of worship and a way of acknowledging and praising God for all that He has done. We have been given so much that praise and generosity should be our natural response when we recognize all that God has done for us (Colossians 1:12-14, Psalm 103:1-5). Giving back to Him is just a small acknowledgment that He has given us everything—even His only Son. And it is all of who He is and all of what He has done that should compel us to worship Him in the way that He has prescribed.

"Giving back to Him is just a small acknowledgment that He has given us everything—even His only Son."

Reflect on the things that God has given you, both material and eternal. What are some of the ways you can give to God out of a gracious heart in thanksgiving for all that He has done?

In Deuteronomy 26:18, we are yet again reminded of the covenant that God has made with Israel. What are some ways that you find yourself encouraged by the repetition of Scripture?

Read Colossians 1:12-14 and Psalm 103:1-5. Spend some time in prayerful thanksgiving to the Lord for all that He has done for us.

Deuteronomy 28-30

Deuteronomy 28 is a pivotal chapter in the Old Testament. It sets up an explanation for many of the events that will follow in the rest of the Old Testament books and the history of the nation of Israel.

It is in this chapter that we see blessings promised for obedience and consequences for disobedience. It is also in this chapter that we can see a sad explanation for the consequences that the people of Israel would face because of their sin.

Our God is a God of redemption. He delights in our obedience, but He also delights in our redemption because of His great love for us. There are blessings for obedience and curses for disobedience. God rewards those who keep the law and serve the Lord with their whole hearts. And those that do not serve the Lord face consequences. But it is the character of God that is demonstrated so greatly in these chapters. He pours out steadfast love on His people. He cares for His children so much, and we are reminded that as they traveled through the wilderness, even their clothing and shoes did not wear out for forty years. The people never lacked. God was faithful through every step of the desert path.

The beginning of chapter 30 gives us a sweet glimpse into who God is. He promises His people that if they return to Him, He will redeem them. The chapter ends with a call to choose life and the Lord. Despite the fact that the world tries to convince us that we will find peace in what it offers, He is the only thing that satisfies. Even when our hearts wander, He is always ready and waiting to redeem and restore. His steadfast love pursues us, and His heart's desire is always for us to run back to Him. This is good news for our wandering hearts.

"Even when our hearts wander, He is always ready and waiting to redeem and restore."

How does chapter 28 expand your understanding of the rest of the Old Testament?

Think about how throughout wandering for forty years, the Israelites never lacked anything—God always provided for them. Write a list below of how God has provided for you in ways that you did not expect.

As you read chapter 30, write a list of aspects of God's character. What are some things that you have learned about God's character through reading Deuteronomy?

Deuteronomy 31-34

As we come to the end of the book of Deuteronomy, we also come to the end of Moses's life.

Moses had been the strong and courageous leader of the nation of Israel for decades, and now it is the end of His life. He has trained and encouraged his successor Joshua. Moses uses his final days to praise the Lord, bless the nation of Israel, and encourage them to be faithful to the Lord who has delivered them and pursued their hearts.

His words in Deuteronomy 31:8 remind the people, and us, that our God will never leave us. He walks with us every step of the way. But the final words of Moses are also full of warning as God reveals to him that the people of Israel will indeed rebel. Moses finds comfort and peace in the steadfast character of the God He knows intimately.

At the very end of the book of Deuteronomy, the impact of Moses on the nation of Israel is evident, but Deuteronomy 34:10 says that Moses was a man who the Lord knew face to face. What a privilege and an honor to know the Lord so intimately. Moses was not a perfect man, but he loved the Lord and served Him with his life. His life is a reminder to us to seek intimacy with the Lord and serve Him with our lives. The death of Moses without entering the Promised Land is a sad reminder to us of the consequences and seriousness of sin. Moses would die before entering into the land of promise, and he would die clinging to the hope of the promised Messiah. How sweet it is then to read Matthew 17 and know that Moses is with Jesus at the transfiguration. More than that, the transfiguration takes place in the Promised Land. While scholars debate whether Moses actually "saw" the Promised Land during the transfiguration, one thing is clear: God restores what was once lost. God gave Moses something much better than the Promised Land; He gave him the Messiah. God had been faithful to Moses, and we know that He will be faithful to us as well.

"God restores what was once lost."

Take a moment to reread Deuteronomy 31:8. How does your confidence in the Lord grow through reading this verse?

Some of Moses's last actions that are described in chapters 33 and 34 are giving praise to God and instructing the Israelites. How does this encourage you to be steadfast in praise to God and serving others despite your circumstances?

Reflect on the fact that God knew Moses face to face. Spend some time in prayer, and ask God to allow you to have a more intimate relationship with Him.

Worship Him
in sincerity
and truth.

Joshua

GENRE: Historical Narrative

AUTHOR / DATE WRITTEN

Unknown, likely Joshua • c. 1380-1370 BC

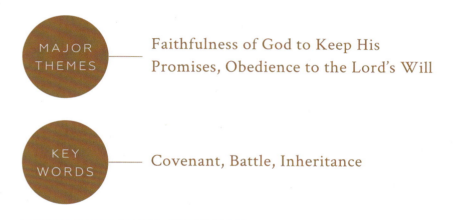

MAJOR THEMES — Faithfulness of God to Keep His Promises, Obedience to the Lord's Will

KEY WORDS — Covenant, Battle, Inheritance

KEY VERSES

JOSHUA 24:14-15

Therefore, fear the Lord and worship him in sincerity and truth. Get rid of the gods your fathers worshiped beyond the Euphrates River and in Egypt, and worship the Lord. But if it doesn't please you to worship the Lord, choose for yourselves today: Which will you worship — the gods your fathers worshiped beyond the Euphrates River or the gods of the Amorites in whose land you are living? As for me and my family, we will worship the Lord.

Joshua 1-3

The book of Joshua is a book filled with God's faithfulness to His people.

He will always do what He has said that He will do. The Lord commissions Joshua and promises to be with Him. He also exhorts Joshua to be strong and courageous and to dwell and meditate on God's Word. The first chapter of the book is key as the Lord commands the people not to depart from the Word of the Lord. As they entered into the Promised Land, the temptation would be to try to live in their own strength and forget to teach the Scripture to their children as they had been commanded in Deuteronomy 6. The people promised to follow the Lord and follow Joshua, but we know that they will not do this perfectly.

Chapter 2 introduces us to an unlikely heroine, Rahab, the harlot. She is not exactly considered important in her society, and yet God uses her greatly. She hides the two spies from the wicked king, and verse 11 contains her proclamation of faith in the Lord. This unlikely heroin heard of the God of Israel and all that He has done, and she places her faith in the one true God. She would see His steadfast love poured out on her and her family. She was not the kind of person who would have been expected to be part of the conquest of the Promised Land, but God showed grace to her. In fact, when we open the New Testament and read the genealogy of Jesus, we find the name of Rahab listed in the family tree of the Messiah. Her life is a demonstration of the grace of God.

In chapter 3, the time has finally come to cross over the Jordan and into the Promised Land. The waters parted once all of the priests dipped their feet in the water. What a sweet reminder that so often, we need to step out in faith to see the amazing things that the Lord wants to do. God had done what He had promised to His people. He had been faithful to deliver them and faithful to bring them through the wilderness, and His faithful pursuit and covenant blessings would continue.

"God had done what He had promised to His people."

God repetitively instructs Joshua to "be strong and courageous." How does God's character give Joshua the confidence to be strong and courageous?

Think about the unlikeliness, by worldly standards, of God using Rahab in His plans. How does this grow your understanding of God's power and His graciousness?

In Joshua 3:7, the Lord tells Joshua that He will exalt him in order to prove to Israel that He will remain with Joshua. What are some ways that the Lord has exalted you so that others can see and know Him better?

Joshua 4-6

Just as there had been an exodus out of Egypt and through the Red Sea, we see here a mini exodus as the Israelites cross through the Jordan River and into the land of Canaan.

God kept His promises to bring them into this good land, and they are commanded to set up stones of remembrance and teach the generations who follow about the faithfulness of their covenant-keeping God. The men would then be circumcised as a reminder of God's covenant promises, and the Passover would be celebrated for the first time in the Promised Land. The close of chapter 5 reveals the commander of the Lord's army. This is likely a pre-incarnate manifestation of Jesus and a reminder of who would fight the battles ahead.

We come to the iconic story of the battle of Jericho, where the walls fall, and the city is defeated by the Israelites circling the city and blowing trumpets. God had already won the battle, and He wants His people to demonstrate their faith to themselves and the world so that all would know that He is Lord.

Chapter 6 takes us back to the story of Rahab. The city was destroyed, but one woman and her family were saved. She may seem like an unlikely choice, the prostitute saved by her faith. But that is how the Lord works—saving sinners and using them for His glory. Rahab is mentioned several times in Scripture. She is commended for her faith (James 2:25, Hebrews 11:31) and is honored as a woman who feared the Lord more than men. But it is her position in the genealogy of Jesus that is such a beautiful picture of redemption (Matthew 1:5). God took a woman who was an outcast of society and made her an important part of the family tree of Jesus. His grace was abundant in her life. He used her, and He desires to use you as well.

"That is how the Lord works—saving sinners and using them for His glory."

In chapter 4, we read about the stones of remembrance, physical reminders of how the Lord accomplished things on behalf of Israel. What are some physical reminders that you might surround yourself with that testify to what the Lord has done?

The Lord accomplished the destruction of Jericho in a seemingly unconventional way. How does this expand your understanding of how God orchestrates things in strange ways so that He may receive more glory?

Rahab and her family were spared from the destruction of Jericho because of her faith that the Israelites' God was the one true God. She is described as a harlot, and yet we see that she was used in the lineage of Christ. She is an example of someone justified by Christ, and she is considered a hero of the faith. Despite how the world might have described her, Christ identifies her as a child of God. How does this encourage you when you think about your own identity?

Joshua 7-9

As the nation of Israel fights to claim the Promised Land, we are reminded that one person's sin can affect many.

There is nothing in our lives that is outside of the reach of His redeeming hand.

Achan disobeyed the Lord, and he thought that he had hidden his sin. But with the Lord, nothing is hidden. God saw what he had done, and the entire nation paid for Achan's sin against the Lord and against the nation. The place the sin happened is named the Valley of Achor, which means the Valley of Trouble.

The Valley of Achor is mentioned one more time in Scripture when the Lord says that the Valley of Achor will be a gateway of hope (Hosea 2:15). It is a beautiful picture of redemption that only the Lord can bring. He takes the Valley of Trouble and makes it a gateway of hope. He can redeem and restore anything in our lives as well. There is nothing in our lives that is outside of the reach of His redeeming hand. He is the God of redemption.

The sin of this one man impacted many in the nation of Israel. This far-reaching sin reminds us of the sin of Adam that plummeted the world into depravity. But it also reminds us of the righteousness of Christ. For it is through this one man that many will be made righteous (Romans 5:12-21). The condemnation that comes through the fall cannot compare to the redemption that comes through Christ.

Achan chose to break the covenant, and he would bear the consequences of that action. The next chapters detail for us the battles and situations the people of Israel would face as they came into the land that God had promised them. They were in the Promised Land, and yet there were still trials and the need to rehearse and remember all that God had done for them. Chapter 9 shows how they needed to go to the Lord for direction in everything. The stories of conquest and Canaan may seem distant to us, but as the people of God, we can learn much about God's character and what it means to serve Him.

144

In Joshua 7:21, we see that Achan broke the covenant that Israel had with the Lord for a cloak and some gold and silver. Even as Christians, we often betray God for things much less valuable. Below, list some things that you might allow to sell your faith short. Spend some time in prayer, thanking God for His graciousness and asking for His strength to desire Him more fully.

Reread Joshua 8:34. As a part of renewing their commitment to the Law, Joshua read the whole Law to them aloud. How does this expand your understanding of the importance of Scripture reading?

Although the Gibeonites were deceptive in their covenant, Israel still kept their oath. How is this reflective of how God keeps His covenants with us? How does this grow your understanding of the importance of a covenant?

Joshua 10-12

God is faithful to His people. He keeps His covenants, and He does what He says He will do.

Chapter 10 details the battle at Gibeon and how Joshua cries out to the Lord and fervently pleads for the sun to stand still. And it does. God makes the sun and the moon stop until the Israelites have won the battle. The Lord fought for Israel and answered the plea of Joshua. What a reminder for us to pray and to come boldly before the Lord (Hebrews 4:16). God was fighting for His people, and He heard the prayer of Joshua. The Israelites won the battles because of the Lord. He is the great victor and hero of each story.

The rest of the passage is also full of reminders of His faithfulness. In chapter 11, the people finally pass into the land that God had promised to Abraham in Genesis 15. We may not always understand God's plan or His timing, but He always does what He says He will do. He is faithful to His children. He can cause the sun to stand still, and He can certainly take care of you and me. Faithfulness is who He is.

At first glance, the last chapter may seem insignificant to us. It is a list of the kings who were conquered under the leadership of Moses and Joshua. But a bigger point is being made by the author because these kings were not just conquered by Moses, Joshua, or even by the army of Israel — they were conquered by Jesus. Jesus is the King of kings. He is greater than any king who has ever been and any king who will ever be. He is sovereign over history, and He will never fail. The nation of Israel seemed small and weak, but God used them to accomplish His purpose. Jesus came, small and seemingly weak as a baby in a manger, but the baby in the manger was also the King over all kings. He is our faithful King. And even when things do not seem to make sense, we can trust that His ways are not ours. He keeps His covenants with His people. He does what He says He will do.

Joshua's plea to God for the sun and moon to stand still is bold.
What does this teach us about God's power? What does it teach us
about asking in faith for Him to provide?

In chapter 11, the Israelites finally inhabit the land that the Lord promised to
Moses. Reread the last verse of the chapter. Joshua took the entirety of the land
because he was obedient to all that the Lord told Moses. What does this reveal
about the importance of obedience to God?

Chapter 12 lists the kings who Israel struck down—a list totaling 31 kings.
How does this encourage you in the knowledge that God delivers us
from those who oppose Him?

Joshua 13-15

God's faithfulness is seen again and again in the book of Joshua.

Over and over, we see that God does what He says He will do. Tucked into verse 6 of chapter 13, we are reminded that it is the Lord who is fighting the battles for His people and that He rewards the faithful obedience of His children. He would be faithful in the future, just as He had been faithful to His people in the past.

Chapter 14 reintroduces Caleb, who has been mentioned throughout the story of God's people. Caleb had been one of the two spies years ago who had given a good report, and he had waited to receive the land God had promised to him. He is now 85 years old when we are reintroduced to him, but the constant testimony of his life is that he was a man who followed the Lord. No matter what the people around him did, Caleb was faithful to the Lord. He is a picture of faithfulness and perseverance. God kept His promise to Caleb. Caleb received the inheritance that he had been promised. Our God is trustworthy. He will do what He has said He will do.

The reminders of God's faithfulness throughout the biblical narrative encourage us to trust Him to provide. Specifically, they urge us to trust in His provision of the Messiah. Each step of the way, God's covenant faithfulness to the nation of Israel should have been reminding them that just as He had been faithful to His promise to Abraham to make a great nation and bring them into the land, He would be faithful to bring the Promised One.

We now read the story knowing that God was indeed faithful to that promise. How much more should we be encouraged to trust Him and, like Caleb, live lives devoted to following the Lord.

"Our God is trustworthy. He will do what He has said He will do."

Meditate on Joshua 13:6. How does knowing the Lord will always fight battles for His people refresh your affection for the Lord?

When 45 years have passed, we see Caleb's faithfulness rewarded in a very tangible way. How does this encourage you to continue on in faithfulness to the Lord, even when we must wait for our inheritance in heaven?

Chapter 15 describes historical boundaries. These would have been occupied by real people who had waited for this promise. How does this show you that God cares about the details in the lives of His people?

Joshua 16-18

In these first chapters, we see the land boundaries given. Sadly, we also see that the people did not completely obey the words of Joshua or what Moses had commanded before him, and they did not drive out the Canaanites. We are not told exactly why they did not obey, but it appears that they did not trust the Lord to do what He promised He would do, though He had proven Himself faithful at every turn.

In a beautiful picture of all that God had done, the tabernacle is set up for the first time in the Promised Land. It is placed in Shiloh and is a reminder that God has given the land and fulfilled the promise He made so many years before. The Tent of Meeting housed the presence of God among His people and pointed to Jesus who would come and tabernacle, or dwell, among His people.

At the beginning of chapter 18, Joshua reminds the people that they need to go in and possess the land. They needed to take what God had already given to them. They needed to trust that His promises were true and live in response to what He had done. Psalm 16:5-6 is a beautiful reference to what we see taking place here in Joshua, and it is a reminder to us that the Lord Himself is our portion. The boundary lines have been drawn, and we have been given a beautiful inheritance. We have been given Him, and He is the greatest inheritance we could have ever hoped for.

"The Lord Himself is our portion."

In Chapter 17, we see that Joseph's descendants demand additional land because of the size of their tribe. Joshua tells them to drive out the Canaanites, yet they fail to do so. How does this expand your understanding that partial obedience is disobedience?

Joshua 18:3 describes Joshua urging the Israelites to take possession of the land that God had given them. How does this encourage you to be bold in your faith?

Take a moment to read Psalm 16:5-6. What are some ways that this passage encourages you in your understanding of what Israel was experiencing?

Joshua 19-21

It is within these chapters that the inheritance of the different people groups is listed.

It is also here that we again learn about the cities of refuge, which point us to the great refuge that we find in Jesus. God is our refuge and our strength (Psalm 91:2), and it is only through Jesus that we are able to find refuge from our guilt and sin. The cities of refuge and the inheritances that were given to the people were historical events in the nation of Israel. Still, they also served as pictures pointing us forward to greater realities found in Jesus.

The end of chapter 21 gives us a beautiful reminder of who God is and all that He has done. The people are given rest. They had worked, and the work was good, and now they rest. Not one of their enemies had defeated them, and not one of the Lord's promises had failed. It had been a long and tiring journey, but God had done what He said He would do. He had kept His covenant promises. He had been faithful. He had brought the people up out of Egypt and delivered them through the wilderness wandering, and now He had faithfully brought them to the Promised Land. Even though the people had not always been faithful through this journey, the Lord had been faithful through every moment. He had not failed even one of His promises. The journey may not have looked like what they had expected, but He had done what He had promised.

God is faithful to His people, and He will be faithful to you. We can read this passage and find confidence in Him. He did not fail the nation of Israel, and He will not fail us. He will not let the enemy defeat you, and He will keep every word of His promises (Joshua 21:45). He will never let you down. He will enable you to persevere and endure. The God of hope is our hope for every moment.

"God is faithful to His people, and He will be faithful to you."

QUESTIONS

Chapter 19 lists the inheritances of different tribes of Israel. Think about our inheritance in Christ as believers in Him. List out some ways that our covenant with Christ and our inheritance with Him differs and is similar to what ancient Israel was experiencing during this time.

Cities of refuge are a display of mercy. How does this exemplify the mercy that God shows us?

Reread the very last verse of chapter 21. How can this provide you comfort in your everyday life?

Joshua 22-24

The people have entered the Promised Land as the book of Joshua is about to come to a close.

Joshua gave a final admonition to the people before his death, and the message is simple—serve the Lord. He gives this admonition in Joshua 22:5 for the people to love the law and walk in the ways of God. Above all, Joshua commands the Israelites to love the Lord with all of their hearts and souls, clinging to Him and serving Him forever. In Joshua 23:14-16, Joshua reminds the people that God kept every promise and remained faithful to His covenant. He again gave a reminder that there would be great consequences for covenant disobedience.

Chapter 24 contains the covenant renewal. As part of this gathering, the people would rehearse the faithfulness of God in the past by remembering the events of Genesis, Exodus, and Numbers. As they looked back on all that God had done for them, how could they serve anyone but the Lord? Looking back on all God has done encourages our faith as we are reminded of the faithfulness of our God. The response of our hearts when we see who God is should be to praise Him and Him alone.

Today's reading contains the famous words of Joshua 24:15. Joshua reminded the people of all God had done to rescue and deliver them, and then He urged them to make a choice to serve the Lord above all else. The people were sure they could keep the words of the covenant, and they promised to do it. The problem was that in our own strength, we could not keep the law of God. But the impossibility of us keeping the law points us to our great need for a Savior. Jesus has done what we could never do on our own.

"Jesus has done what we could never do on our own."

In Joshua 23:14, Joshua reminded the people that God had not failed one of His promises. What does that teach you about the character of God? How does that encourage you?

In chapter 24, the people rehearse the faithfulness of God to them in the past. God's faithfulness in the past is a good reminder that He will be faithful now and in the future. How has God been faithful in your life?

Now that we have finished the book of Joshua, write out some of the ways you have seen your understanding of God's character grow. How has your relationship deepened from seeing how God accomplished His promises to Israel?

There was
no king
in Israel.

Judges

GENRE: Historical Narrative

AUTHOR / DATE WRITTEN
Samuel, then Nathan & Gad • c. 1050-1000 BC

MAJOR THEMES — Israel's Endemic Sin, Corrupt Rulers, God's Longsuffering and Justice

KEY WORDS — Wickedness, Rebellion, Exile

KEY VERSE

JUDGES 21:25

In those days there was no king in Israel;
everyone did whatever seemed right to him.

Judges 1-3

The book of Judges picks up where the book of Joshua leaves off.

Unfortunately, in the book of Judges, we will see the rebellion of Israel and their desire to do what is right in their own eyes. God gave clear instructions to drive out the foreign nations and gods from the land that He has given them, and the people fail to obey. God has done so much for the people, and yet they rebel against Him.

The people demonstrated covenant unfaithfulness by walking away from the Lord. The problem in Israel was so great during this time that Judges 2:10 tells us that after Joshua died, a generation arose who did not know the Lord or what He had done for Israel. After all that we have seen God do for the people, it seems almost impossible that they did not pass on to their children the message of Yahweh. The people failed to keep the words of the Shema in Deuteronomy 6:4-9 and the command that Joshua had given in Joshua 1.

As a result of Israel's disobedience, the Lord raised up judges in the land to rule the people, and throughout the book of Judges, they are pictures to point us back to Jesus. Othniel, Ehud, and Shamgar are human judges who point us to a greater judge. Jesus is the long-awaited and yet unexpected Redeemer. Even in the sometimes confusing and difficult passages of Judges, God is at work. The story of redemption is seen from the first page to the last. Jesus is on every page.

"The story of redemption is seen from the first page to the last."

In chapter 1, we see that Judah and Simeon lead Israel in defeating 10,000 men by God's strength. How does this exemplify that God uses our weaknesses to reveal and prove His great strength?

Chapter 2 describes that as future Israelite generations came along, they had forgotten the many ways that God had continued to provide for them. How does this encourage you to live a life that testifies the goodness of God to younger generations?

Because Ehud was left-handed, his sword was unable to be detected when searched by the king's servants. How does this expand your understanding of how God uses our odd traits to accomplish His plans?

Judges 4-6

In these chapters, we meet two women who stand up and do what is right.

Deborah is a judge and prophetess. She is a brave and faithful woman who goes with Barak up to battle and proclaims that God will give the evil Sisera into the hand of a woman. Jael is that woman. The evil Sisera comes to her tent, and, in bravery, she kills him while risking her own life. She fights for the Lord with the weapon that she has in her tent. She did what she could and used what she had. In the beautiful song of Deborah and Barak, they praise the Lord for all He has done. Deborah is named as a mother of Israel, and Jael is listed as a heroine and blessed among women.

God so often uses the most unlikely people to bring Him glory. These women were living in a time when women were not highly revered, yet God used them. He uses people who will serve Him right where they are and do what He has called them to do. Deborah and Jael remind us that God will use each of us with our specific strengths right in the place that He has called.

As we move into chapter 6, we are introduced to Gideon. Gideon would be used by God as well, though he also did not seem like the most likely candidate for the task set before him. Gideon was far from a perfect man. He stumbled and asked for signs, and yet God was faithful to use Gideon. God's strength shone through Gideon's weakness. Though the judges we meet in this book are imperfect, they point us toward the perfect judge who would come in Christ.

"God will use each of us with our specific strengths right in the place that He has called."

Reread the interaction between Barak and Deborah in Judges 4:6-10.
We see Deborah wholeheartedly trusting that what the Lord says is true.
In what ways can you be more like Deborah in this respect?

Spend a moment reflecting on how God used both Jael and Deborah.
What are some ways these women encourage you to pursue obedience
to the Lord in your unique womanhood?

In chapter 6, Gideon is concerned that he is the youngest in his family and
that his family is the weakest in Manasseh. Despite this, the Lord still ordains
him as judge over Israel. How can this encourage you to obey God in boldness
for what He has told you to do?

Judges 7-9

The book of Judges shows that God uses imperfect people.

Gideon is an example of an imperfect man who God used for His glory. The Lord called Gideon, and he immediately lacked faith and asked for signs. Yet God was patient with him. It is so often in our weakness that we see the strength of the Lord and His power in us (2 Corinthians 12:9). In chapter 7, God uses only 300 men of the army of Israel. God is teaching them that it is His power and not our own. Victory is all because of who He is. If God had sent an army of thousands, the people would have been tempted to think that they had won the battle in their own strength, but by using just a few hundred men, God made it clear that victory comes only through Him. He was at work for His people that day, and He was teaching them to trust in His steadfast hand.

We do not look to Gideon as an example of what we should be because he had many failures. Instead, we look to Gideon's God, who never fails. God used an imperfect and doubting man, and He will use us as well. No matter where we are or how little it seems we have to offer, God can use us right where we are for His glory. God does not always work in the way that we expect that He will. He uses the unexpected to bring about His plan. This same truth would be seen in Jesus, who would come as the Messiah. The people were expecting a conquering ruler who would overthrow the political forces of the day, but instead, Jesus came to capture the hearts of His people and to overthrow the religion of self-sufficiency to which we are so prone. God wants us to know that it is His grace alone that rescues His people.

"God wants us to know that it is His grace alone that rescues His people."

In Judges 7:2, the Lord clearly explains that He wants fewer troops sent into battle against the Midianites. What are some of the ways that you have seen God's strength perfected in your weaknesses?

At the end of chapter 8, we see another instance of Israel's forgetfulness of God's provision and care for them. In what ways do you struggle to remember God's provision for you? What are some practical steps to flee from this sin?

Abimelech did not trust the processes and plans of God and took matters into his own hands to ensure he would rule over Israel. However, we see that God punishes him for this. What does this tell us about God's steadfastness in His plans? How can this comfort you?

Judges 10-12

Things have become dire in Israel as the people continue to do what is right in their own eyes.

"We must allow God to change our hearts so that our words will be changed as well."

They continue to forsake God and turn to the gods of the heathen nations. Though the Lord rescued His people from Egypt and brought them into the Promised Land, the people turned to idols. At the end of chapter 10, we feel the weight of this decision as God speaks to the people and tells them to let the idols that they had chosen save them. Of course, these idols, made by the hands of men, had no power to save anyone. The fact that the people were running after idols was a clear picture of the people's hearts.

In Jephthah, we are reminded of the power of our words and specifically of words that overflow from what is in our hearts. Jephthah makes a rash and tragic vow that he will sacrifice whatever comes out of the door of his house. When his own daughter comes out of that door, he does not repent of this foolish vow, but in selfishness, he is more concerned about himself and his own reputation than he is of his daughter. Our words are powerful, and the heart behind the words that we speak is also powerful. We must allow God to change our hearts so that our words will be changed as well.

Sin with our words and the idols of our hearts are not foreign to us. These issues that we scoff at the people of Israel for having so often reside in our own sin-stricken hearts as well. We run to idols, looking for satisfaction when it is our Creator who has delivered us. We sin against others with our words, and we follow the desires of our sinful hearts. The book of Judges is heavy and raw, and it reveals the sinful tendencies of our own hearts. But it also points us to Jesus, who is the only judge who is able to rescue us.

Spend some time in reflection about your own words. In what ways can you relate to Jephthah's foolish vow? Take some time to pray for the words that may come from your mouth—that they would be edifying to those around you and glorifying to God.

Judges 10:14 is a sobering remark made by God. Do you find yourself only going to God when you need something? What are some ways that you can more appropriately and continually hold fast to the Lord?

In chapter 10, we see the Israelites once again return to sinful ways and abandon God, yet God never abandons them. How does this grow your understanding of God's character?

Judges 13-15

These chapters introduce us to Samson, who is one of the most well-known judges in Scripture.

Samson was the twelfth of Israel's judges, and he would be the final judge. These chapters and the story of Samson open with the people of Israel being unfaithful yet again. The story quickly shifts, and we see Samson is set apart and given a Nazirite vow from birth. We would expect someone who had been set apart for the Lord to live a life of service and praise to the Lord, but instead, Samson is constantly living out his own will and desires. He marries a Philistine woman even though his parents discourage it. He is deceitful and pushes the limits of his own vow, and he also takes credit for the victories that God has given. When God gives him supernatural power, Samson sings praises to himself about the accomplishments that he attributed to himself instead of praising the Lord for all that He had done.

As we learn about Samson, we easily become frustrated by his pride and self-centered attitude, but God continues showing grace to him. Samson was selfish, and he thought that he was self-sufficient. He failed to recognize that everything he accomplished was by the mercy of God and a demonstration of His steadfast love. However, it is a reminder to us of the grace that we have been given. So often, we live in pride and self-centeredness as Samson did, undeserving of all God has done for us, but the Lord continues to pour out His grace.

Samson was the last judge in the period of the judges. His flawed life leaves us longing for a judge to come who would rule rightly. In the life of Samson, we see a miraculous birth and one that is set apart. Most of all, we see a man commissioned by God to save his people. Samson's life is both a picture of our need and a glimpse of the One who will perfectly fulfill the role of judge. Samson points us to Jesus.

"We are so undeserving of all that He has done for us, yet He continues pouring out His grace."

Reread Judges 13:18. Think about how the angel of the Lord (God Himself) proclaims that His name is beyond understanding. What are some ways your understanding of God has grown since you have begun reading through the Old Testament? Take some time in prayer to thank God for allowing you to take a mere glimpse at who He is and the power of His name.

Samson delighted in his strength rather than praising God for His provision of strength to him. Take some time in self-examination. How often do you find yourself doing similar things?

Throughout this reading, we see God being incredibly gracious and long-suffering with Samson. How has reading this passage expanded your understanding of God's nature?

Judges 16-18

The end of Samson's life is found in chapter 16, and it is a tragic account that draws his story to a close.

In this chapter, we see Samson chasing after Philistine women yet again, and we are introduced to a prostitute, Delilah. Delilah conspires against Samson to defeat him with the Philistines, and though she tries multiple times, Samson lies to her. It seems that Samson felt invincible. When he finally shares that his hair had never been cut, he is besieged by the Philistines. Samson's true strength was not in his hair but in the power of the Lord. Sadly, Samson did not even notice when the Lord left him in Judges 16:20. Despite Samson's life of selfishness and pride, God would use him to defeat the Philistines, and his name would even be recorded in Hebrews 11:32. God, in His mercy and grace, had used Samson's weakness for His glory.

The next chapters remind us not to place our identity in things. We are reminded of how often we long after things that are not our own. We are introduced to Micah, and immediately we learn how he clings to things and is covetous of what others have. There are many things that Micah wants, and when he wants something, he goes and takes it. But at the end of chapter 18, after he has taken the things he wanted, he loses everything that means so much to him. He is left in despair because the things and idols he treasures so much are taken from him.

We often build our lives around idols as well. We exalt things to such prominent places in our lives that we do not know what we would do or how we would go on without them. What a reminder to place our hope in Christ alone. This world is uncertain, but our God is sure. Let us build our lives around Him alone. Let us come humbly before Him. Let us remind our hearts that He is more important than anything else this world has to offer.

"Let us build our lives around Him alone."

In Judges 16:28, we read that Samson called out to God for strength to defeat his enemies after his hair had been cut. God provides the strength, and Samson is able to accomplish more in his death than in his whole life. How does the understanding that Samson's strength was only in God and not in his hair expand your understanding of God's strength and power?

Chapter 17 describes Micah's extreme departure from obedience to the Lord. How does your reading of Leviticus and Deuteronomy help you better understand how this is a provocation of God's holiness and justice?

Reread Judges 18:24. In what ways can you relate to what Micah is saying? And how can we as Christians put all of our affection in God rather than in things we create?

Judges 19-21

The book of Judges does not end triumphantly. The people are living in sin and doing what is right in their own eyes.

The book began showing great honor to women with the daughter of Othniel, Deborah, and Jael. But as the book closes, we learn that women are objectified, mistreated, and abused. This is often the case in cultures that turn from the Lord. The people, along with the judges, made so many mistakes, and the result is a nation spiraling into sin and depravity.

It would be easy to finish this book feeling discouraged. Yet, in Hebrews 11, some of these same judges are listed as people of faith. Hebrews 11:34 tells us that they were made strong out of weakness. God used many of these people despite their sins and shortcomings. God uses weak people to bring Him glory. Instead of finishing Judges feeling discouraged, we can walk away with the hope that just as the Lord used these men of weak faith, He can use us as well. 2 Corinthians 12:9-10 reminds us that God's strength is made perfect in our weakness. The book of Judges gives us reason to rejoice. He works in our weakness. He uses even our weakness for His glory.

Most of all, the book of Judges makes us long for a better judge. Throughout the book, we see the phrase repeated that there was no king in Israel, and though the kingship would soon come to Israel, it is the true messianic King the hearts of the people were longing for. The book of Judges reveals the result of life without a king, and this horrific picture is a reminder to us of what life would be without our true King and Judge.

"God's strength is made perfect in our weakness."

At the end of chapter 19, we see that the Levite man cuts his concubine into twelve pieces to send throughout the tribes of Israel, and though gruesome, we can learn much from this gesture. Reread Judges 20:4-9. The purpose of this was to get Israel's attention and to ensure justice and a turn away from wickedness. How does this teach us to be bold in defending the church against the infiltration of sin?

The very last verse of Judges reiterated what has been said throughout the book. Reflect on what you have learned about doing what is right in your own eyes.

How do we find hope in the gospel despite the sorrowful account of the book of Judges?

and your
God will
be my God.

Ruth

GENRE: **Historical Narrative**

AUTHOR / DATE WRITTEN

Likely Samuel • c. 1011 & 931 BC

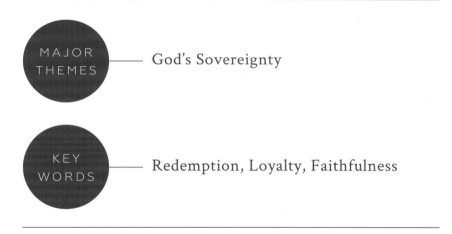

MAJOR THEMES —— God's Sovereignty

KEY WORDS —— Redemption, Loyalty, Faithfulness

KEY VERSE

RUTH 1:16

But Ruth replied: Don't plead with me to abandon you or to return and not follow you. For wherever you go, I will go, and wherever you live, I will live; your people will be my people, and your God will be my God.

Ruth 1-4

The book of Ruth takes place during the time of the judges. It is a glimmer of grace during a dark time.

It is the story of redemption in four short chapters. The book begins with a Jewish man named Elimelech who takes his family to Moab to escape a famine. Elimelech and his two sons, Mahlon and Chilion, die in Moab, leaving Elimelech's wife, Naomi, and his son's wives, Ruth and Orpah, as widows. Ruth is a foreign woman who became a widow—quite a scary position to fall into in this culture, but Ruth puts her faith in the God of Israel when she follows her mother-in-law, Naomi, back to Bethlehem. As a poor widow who is completely helpless, she meets Boaz, who becomes her kinsman-redeemer. Boaz shows grace to Ruth and Naomi. Boaz pursues Ruth and pays a high price to redeem her.

The entire story of Ruth teaches us how God sovereignly and providentially works in the lives of His people. Boaz points us to Jesus. He is a picture of Jesus, who is our true and better kinsman-redeemer. Boaz showed grace to Ruth as Jesus shows grace to us. Ruth was a foreign woman just as we are foreigners to God's covenant grace, but God has spread His arms of grace wide open to make us a part of His family and citizens of heaven (Ephesians 2:12-13, 19). As Ruth came to Boaz poor and helpless, so we come poor and needy to the Lord who is the only one who can save.

The last verses of the book remind us again of our God's power of redemption. We learn that Boaz is the son of another foreign woman, Rahab, the prostitute who turned to God (Joshua 2). And it would be through this line that God would bring David and ultimately Jesus. God was working to bring about His sovereign plan, even when things seemed desperate. The book of Ruth reminds us to trust the Redeemer.

"God was working to bring about His sovereign plan, even when things seemed desperate."

Ruth exhibits an incredible amount of loyalty toward Naomi. How does this encourage you to hold fast to other members of the body of Christ?

How does the character of Boaz as the kinsman-redeemer remind you and point you to Christ?

In Genesis, we read many genealogies, and now we read about Ruth, a woman who is in the genealogy of Christ. How does the preservation of Ruth point to God's plan?

They have
rejected
Me as
their king.

1 Samuel

GENRE: Historical Narrative

AUTHOR / DATE WRITTEN

Likely Samuel, Nathan, & Gad • c. 1000 BC

MAJOR THEMES — The Desire for a Godly King, Living with Spiritual Integrity and Knowledge of the Lord

KEY WORDS — Kingship, Character, Integrity

KEY VERSE

1 SAMUEL 8:6-7

When they said, "Give us a king to judge us," Samuel considered their demand wrong, so he prayed to the Lord. But the Lord told him, "Listen to the people and everything they say to you. They have not rejected you; they have rejected me as their king."

I Samuel 1-3

The book of 1 Samuel begins with Hannah's story and the child she prays for.

Hannah is a broken woman who so desperately desires a child. She takes her sorrow and longing to the Lord, and she pours out her heart before Him (Psalm 62:8, Psalm 142:1-3). She promises the Lord that if she is given a child, she will dedicate him to the Lord. God answers her request, and she keeps the promise she has made. And though taking Samuel to the temple must have broken her heart, we still see her praise the Lord through her beautiful prayer in Chapter 2, thanking God for His faithfulness and who He is. Her prayer bears a striking resemblance to the prayer that Mary would pray in Luke 1:46-55.

We know from our study thus far that the nation was in a place of disobedience, and the household of Eli, who is the high priest, is full of corruption as well. There would be a great judgment that would come because of the rampant sin in everyone, from the common people to those in the high priest's family.

I Samuel 3:1 tells us that the word of the Lord was rare in those days. And yet, we see the Lord of creation speak to a young boy. The Lord speaks, and the young boy, Samuel, obeys. And Hannah's obedience turns out to play a key part in how the Lord would work to raise up a prophet for the nation. God used the obedience of a mother and her son to bring the word of the Lord to Israel. God was setting each piece of the story in place to one day bring Jesus.

God has spoken to us as well through the pages of His Word. He has spoken to us through the gospel of Jesus. His grace and love poured out for us compel us to obey His voice. May it be said of us that we heard and obeyed.

"God was setting each piece of the story in place to one day bring Jesus."

Hannah prayed with extreme zeal and transparency. How does this encourage you to cry out to God in the same type of intimacy that Hannah displays?

Hannah took her blessings and gave them back to the Lord. How are you using your blessings in service to and worship of God?

In chapter 3, we see Eli instructing Samuel to listen to the Lord. How does this encourage you to speak truth into others' lives? How does this encourage you to listen to instruction from other Christians?

I Samuel 4-6

During the years as Samuel grew up, the nation did not seek the Lord. In chapter 4, after being defeated by the Philistines in battle, the people use the ark of the covenant as a good luck charm. But God cannot be manipulated. Thus, the Israelites find even greater defeat when they try to manipulate the Lord. The ark of the Lord, which is the symbol of His presence, is taken by the Philistines. Eli, the priest, dies when he learns of the death of his sons and the capture of the ark. But the ark would teach the Philistines of God's power. The Philistines set up the ark in the temple of their god, but the next morning their great statue is lying on the ground. They propped him back up, but he would soon be found face down again.

The people of Ashdod were afflicted for taking the ark. God will not be manipulated by His own people or by the enemy nations. And eventually, they want rid of the ark so much that they are ready to concoct a plan to send it back. God faithfully used the plans of an enemy nation to return the ark to the people of Israel.

Our God is holy. He is worthy of worship and glory, and He cannot be manipulated by human schemes or mocked by His enemies. At a time in the history of Israel when the people were far from God, they still tried to use Him for their own purposes. The words of 1 Samuel are a sober reminder of the holiness of God and His desire for our obedience in faith. God is not something we use to get what we want. Instead, He longs to be the only desire of our longing hearts.

"Our God is holy."

In chapter 4, the Israelites try to use the ark for their purposes. Because they sought to use God as a weapon in place of a leader, they were not victorious. Spend some time reflecting on whether or not you look to God as your weapon or as your leader.

God shows Himself and His greatness to the Philistines through repeatedly making their god fall on his face. In what ways has God shown Himself strong in your life? Are you allowing Him to tear down the idols that might exist in your own heart?

Because the people of Ashdod had taken hold of the ark, God heavily afflicted them. How does this expand your understanding of God's holiness?

I Samuel 7-9

Though the Lord had given the people everything they needed, they looked around at the nations and desired what others had.

Samuel was set apart from the judges we studied in the book of Judges. In chapter 7, the people recognize their sin as Samuel judges the people. Samuel was a transitional figure in Israel as he was both a judge and a spiritual leader. But the people are not happy with the way God has ordered things. They wanted a king like the other nations had. Their sin was not simply in asking for a king but in rejecting the Lord. God had given detailed instructions for kings in Deuteronomy 17:14-20, and if we look at that passage, we see that God sovereignly knew exactly what the people would demand. He knew that the people would desire a king, and He gave specific laws for what kind of man should be a king.

God had chosen and set the nation of Israel apart to serve Him and follow Him (Deuteronomy 7:6-11). He had promised covenant blessings if they would obey the covenant and consequences if they would rebel. God was their great King, but the people were too blinded by their sin to see that. The people wanted a king to do what God would have done if they had been faithful to the covenant. The people wanted covenant blessings without the Lord. I Samuel 8:19-20 tells us that the people want a king like the other nations — someone who would judge them, go before them, and fight their battles. God had done this for them time and time again. He had brought them out of Egypt and fought battles that seemed impossible. But now, the people want things their way, and God allows Samuel to do what the people ask.

The people were searching for a king and going about things in all the wrong ways. Yet even through their sinful rebellion, God was working a plan to bring about the true King. God was preparing to bring a messianic King who would be so much more than a political or national leader. Behind the scenes, God was working though no one yet knew what He would do.

"God was their great King, but the people were too blinded by their sin to see that."

In 1 Samuel 7:3-6, we see that deliverance only comes when we are exclusively worshiping God. How does this help keep you accountable to hold the Lord as the highest in your life?

At the beginning of chapter 8, we see Israel reject God as king so that they could be more like the other nations. Spend some time reflecting on how you might also desire the things of the world rather than allegiance to God.

In 1 Samuel 9:20-21, we see again that God uses a seemingly insignificant person to accomplish His will. How does this grow your affections for the Lord?

I Samuel 10-12

The people have demanded a king, and God allows them to have their way.

He gives them Saul who seems to have everything the people could have wanted in a king. Though we will see many positive character traits in Saul, we will also be made aware of his shortcomings and the reasons that he would eventually be rejected as the king of Israel. From the start, Saul is often crippled by the fear of man and self-consciousness that keeps him from doing what God called him to do. He is often a people pleaser who is more concerned with what men think of him than following the Lord.

Saul's life is a reminder to us to not fear men but God alone (Proverbs 29:25). Yet despite the failings of Saul, we see the Lord bring victory through him in chapter 11. We must be careful to see that the salvation that came was fully and completely of the Lord.

In Samuel's final admonition to the people, he reminds the nation of all that God had done for them, and he pleads with them to serve the Lord alone. God had chosen these people, and His heart's desire is for them to serve Him. Samuel reminds the people that they are guilty before the Lord and reminds them of their dependence on the Lord and all that God has done to deliver His people. Samuel reminded them of the covenant promises and covenant consequences. God had been faithful to His people, and that should have compelled them to serve Him, yet they wanted things their way. All that God has done for us in the past should propel us to serve Him with everything we have (1 Samuel 12:24). Samuel gives this admonition to the nation of Israel, and the words hold true for us as well.

"All that God has done for us in the past should propel us to serve Him with everything we have."

QUESTIONS

1 Samuel 10:22 reveals that Saul ran from his inauguration as king, and yet the Lord revealed to the Israelites where he was hiding. Spend some time in reflection on whether or not you are a willing and obedient vessel for the Lord's plan. Does this passage comfort you or make you uncomfortable?

Take the time to read Proverbs 29:25. Do you find yourself fearing man like Saul did or fearing the Lord?

1 Samuel 12:23 says that Samuel would sin if he would cease to pray and instruct Israel. How does this encourage you to be steadfast in your prayer life? How does this encourage you to pour into younger believers?

I Samuel 13-15

He was a man who was quick to make decisions that he thought would benefit himself. In this passage, his weakness plays out in several ways. In chapter 13, we see Saul offer a sacrifice in his own time instead of waiting for Samuel to arrive. He did not want to wait, and he did not want to do things God's way. His disobedience would cost him the kingdom, and the language of Samuel's admonition to him echoes of the words that we will read in the Davidic covenant in 2 Samuel 7. Saul could have had a kingdom and a lineage that would have lasted forever, but his sin would have consequences that were great, just as sin always does.

In chapter 14, Saul makes a rash vow that threatens his son. We continue to see Saul as a man of pride who longs to do things the way that he wants them done. When we come to chapter 15, he keeps spoil from the defeated Amalekites in direct disobedience to the command of God to destroy everything. Saul lived a life characterized by partial obedience, and partial obedience is not obedience at all. It was the Lord who had made Saul the king, but instead of following the Lord's commands to him, Saul chose to listen to the will of the people and his sinful heart. Samuel reminded Saul that to the Lord, obedience is better than sacrifice. When Saul should have been concerned with obedience, he was concerned about himself and his own desires, and Saul's lack of obedience would cost him and the kingdom dearly.

In the midst of this section, there is a glimmer of hope. We are introduced to Saul's son, Jonathan, and his radical faith in the Lord. In 1 Samuel 14:6, Jonathan fully trusts in God's sovereignty. He knows that God could do anything with many or only a few. What a lesson for us to trust our God and His way even when it is not the most popular thing to do. He can bring His plan to pass with much or with little. We must simply trust and obey.

"We must simply trust and obey."

Saul took salvation into his own hands by offering the sacrifice before Samuel arrived to do it. What does this teach you about patience?

Jonathan had a bold understanding of the power of God. How does this encourage you to understand God better? How can you be encouraged by God not being limited by our circumstances?

In 1 Samuel 15:22-23, we see that Saul did not fully obey the Lord and that God prefers obedience over sacrifice. Reflect on what ways you might be giving partial obedience to God.

I Samuel 16-18

"There is no need to fear our inadequacies when we are trusting in the Lord's strength and not our own."

David enters the story as a humble, young shepherd boy, but the young shepherd boy would one day become the shepherd of God's people (Psalm 78:70-72). David was not the logical choice for the king of Israel, but the Lord reminded Samuel that He does not see things the same way that we do. Man looks on the outward appearance, but the Lord looks on the heart. David's older and stronger brothers are passed over for the one who the Lord sees with a pure heart. The anointing of David would set a plan in motion to bring about the Son of David, who would be Jesus Himself. God so often uses the most unexpected means to bring about His plan. Whether a shepherd boy or a baby in a manger, His ways are always higher than our own.

In this passage, we read the famous Sunday school tale of David and Goliath. At a closer glance, we see that the story reveals a young man destined to be the king and who trusts the Lord even when it does not make sense. When other men hide in fear, David is filled with confidence in the Lord and boldly goes into battle. The character of David stands in stark contrast to what we have observed about Saul up until this point. While Saul is fearful of men, David fears God alone. David is a reminder to us to trust the Lord no matter what and to know that even if we feel that we are not the best choice, God has a plan and a purpose for us. There is no need to fear our inadequacies when we are trusting in the Lord's strength and not our own.

The message of this story is not that we can go out and slay our giants; it is that God is the one who saves and delivers. In 1 Samuel 17:47, David speaks to Goliath, revealing the purpose of what was happening that day. It was to prove that it is not swords or spears or even stones that save. It is the Lord alone. Salvation comes through His power and not our own.

How can you be encouraged by the fact that David's older and stronger brothers were passed over because the Lord saw that David was the one with a pure heart?

David had the boldness to take down Goliath, and yet Israel quaked at the sight of him. Take a moment to pray to God, asking Him to strengthen you to obey Him in the same boldness that David did.

David and Jonathan make a covenant, and Jonathan gifts David with his royal attire as a gift from their deep friendship. What are some ways this encourages you to love your own friends within the church with more fervor?

I Samuel 19-21

And it does not take long for Saul's heart to fill with uncontrollable jealousy toward the young shepherd warrior. Saul's emotions erase his rationality and set him in a downward spiral of his own destruction. He is overcome by anger that is fueled by his own selfish desires. Despite the king's attempts to hunt down David, God's plans would not be thwarted. Saul's son, Jonathan, and Michal, who is David's wife, protect David. God's plan will always prevail.

In chapters 19 and 20, we see a picture of covenant friendship between David and Jonathan. Jonathan desires God's will and God's kingdom above his own and chooses to support David even though it will mean losing his claim to the throne. What is seen as foolishness by Saul is true wisdom in God's eyes because Jonathan is not simply supporting his friend, David, but following God's plan. David and Jonathan wept as they were forced to say goodbye to each other for what would prove to be a long journey ahead.

We will continue to see God's provision for David through his entire life, despite David's own sin. In chapter 21, the Lord reminds David of His covenant and presence by feeding him with the "Bread of the Presence" (1 Samuel 21:6). God fed David with the daily bread that he needed as a tangible reminder of His faithfulness to him.

No matter what David faced, God was with him, and we can trust that He will be with us as well. He does not leave His children. Even when we face what seems like impossible circumstances, He is there. These chapters point us to Jesus. He is the better covenant keeper. He is the one who lays down Himself for His friends. He is the greatest friend. He is the Bread of Life. He is the daily provision of His people that allows us never to hunger again.

"He does not leave His children."

QUESTIONS

Saul allows his jealousy of David to dictate the way he acts toward him. Meditate on some ways that your negative emotions might be interfering with your relationships with other believers. Spend some time in prayer, asking God to redeem those relationships in your life.

In what ways do you think God was teaching David to trust Him through these difficult circumstances? How can you trust God in your current situation?

How are you encouraged by God's steadfast faithfulness to David? How does this grow your affections for God?

I Samuel 22-24

David assembles an army of outcasts. The distressed and indebted of society become his people.

This is a picture of Jesus who pursues the outcasts and makes them sons and daughters of God. God was providing for David every step of the journey. From his army of outcasts to the prophet Gad who gives him instruction on what to do next, God was near.

Saul's pride and jealousy continued to push him further and further into sin, and David is sent on the run of his life. Saul was willing to do anything to extinguish David and satisfy his jealous rage, including killing the priests of God. It almost takes our breath away as we realize the depths to which Saul allowed his sin to take him. But even this despicable act has the fragrance of God's mercy in it. With the destruction of the priests, the evilness of man was bringing about the decree of God that Eli's house would be destroyed. Yet, as we see happen throughout Scripture, a faithful remnant of people remains—in this case, through Abiathar.

In the midst of Saul's spiral, David is running to the Lord. Several psalms were written during this time (Psalm 142, 52, 54), and they give us insight into the heart of David as he runs to the Lord and trusts Him no matter what. Chapter 23 shows how David goes to the Lord for wisdom when he does not know what to do, and this should be our first response as well. This chapter also gives us a picture of the encouragement of Jonathan to David to cling to God's plan. God's faithfulness is even seen in chapter 24 when David is tempted to take things into his own hands.

God is faithful to His people, and He always provides at just the right time. Our response should always be to run to the Lord and to be confident in Him. No matter what we are facing, we can be confident in the steadfast love and faithfulness of the Lord. He will never fail us. In this passage, we see that God is the provision and provider. He is the deliverer. He is the protector. Through Jesus and the power of the gospel, God is all of these things for us as well.

"God is faithful to His people, and He always provides at just the right time."

QUESTIONS

Take a moment to reflect on your prior reading about Saul; he went from showing concern for the Lord and His priests to literally killing them. How does this deepen your understanding of the grip sin takes in your life? How does this encourage you to flee from sin?

Reflect on Psalms 142, 52, and 54. David ran to the Lord in times of deep distress through song. What are some ways you can run to the Lord, whether through song, prayer, writing, etc.? How do these disciplines strengthen your walk with God?

David has the opportunity to kill Saul but refrains. What does this teach you about grace? What does this teach you about trusting God to bring about justice?

I Samuel 25-27

This passage opens with the death of the faithful prophet Samuel. We are then quickly introduced to the foolish Nabal and the wise Abigail.

Nabal is a harsh and foolish man, and David rashly decides to kill Nabal and all of his men. Abigail is a wise woman who comes to David interceding for the lives of those David has decided to kill. She is willing to take the weight of their guilt on herself. Abigail's wise words persuade David not to act rashly. Abigail points us to Jesus, who is the true and better Abigail. He is the one who bears the sins of His people and intercedes on their behalf. It is He who restrains evil in the lives of His people. At the end of the chapter, we see the foolish Nabal die and David repent. However, it is not long before we see his sin rear its head again. He takes Abigail as his wife along with Ahinoham. This is in direct conflict with the command in Deuteronomy 17:17 that says that men should not multiply wives for themselves.

It is in these chapters that we see the wilderness temptations of David. Much like the wilderness temptations of Jesus, David is put in situations in which he must rely on God's strength and trust in His Word. After foregoing another chance to kill Saul, David goes to the foreign Gath where he lived and fought with the Philistines. Chapter 27 does not end on a high note for David as he has brought reproach to his people by his violent life on the run.

Many believe that it was during this time that David wrote Psalm 10. David had a unique ability to come before the Lord with complete honesty. He would pour out his heart, doubts, and fears, and then he would essentially preach the goodness of God to himself. We must frequently do the same in our own lives. We can pour out our hearts before the Lord, and then we can run to His Word and remind ourselves that He is good and will never leave us. We can trust that Our God is holy and faithful, and He will never forsake His own.

As we read these passages, we are reminded that even the heroes of the biblical stories leave us longing. We need a true and better king. We need Jesus.

"We need a true and better king. We need Jesus."

194

In what ways can Abigail's actions point us to Jesus, who is the true and better Abigail?

What do you think that God was trying to teach David through these temptations?

Read Psalm 10. How does this passage encourage you to deepen your prayer life with the Lord?

I Samuel 28-31

This tale is full of tragedy and triumph. We see Saul's desperation as he seeks out the witch, or medium, of Endor. The results of this meeting surprise everyone, and Saul learns that he will die the next day. His tragic reign will come to a tragic end.

Chapters 29 and 30 tell us of great trials in David's life but also of a great God who sustains him through it all. David's relationship with the Philistines is taking a sour turn, and back at the camp, things are even worse. When the men return from battle, they learn that the women and children have been taken captive by the Amalekites. David and the people are so distressed that Scripture says they weep until they have no strength to weep any more. However, verse 6 gives an important key. David strengthened himself in the Lord. When there seems to be nowhere to turn, he turns to the only One who can comfort his hurting heart.

As the chapter unfolds, God gives David the victory, and the women and children are retrieved unharmed. This low point in David's life comes right before a great high point because when the page turns, we see David anointed as king. It is a reminder to run to the Lord and strengthen and encourage our hearts in Him alone. No matter what life brings, He is there.

The final chapter of 1 Samuel chronicles the death of Saul and the end of an important era for Israel. In contrast to David, who strengthened himself in the Lord, we see the tragedy of Saul's life come to an end. We also see here the death of Jonathan, and we are reminded of the consequences of Saul's sin. Not just on himself but on his family and the nation as well.

As 1 Samuel comes to a close, we are left longing for a king and for something better for Israel. And though the turn of the page into 2 Samuel will resolve some of these longings, David will fail us as well. The ending of 1 Samuel does not leave us longing for King David but for King Jesus. He is the true and better King.

"No matter what life brings, He is there."

Even when David's people turn against him, David seeks the Lord. How can this strengthen you to remain steadfast in your relationship with God, even when the world seems to persecute you?

Saul's disobedience causes the death of both himself and his sons. What does this teach us about the far reaches of sin in our lives? Do you consider others' well-being when you are tempted to sin?

Throughout this book, we have seen that God's plan cannot be thwarted. Meditate on the comforting fact that God's plan is good and impenetrable.

Your throne will be established forever.

2 Samuel

GENRE: Historical Narrative

AUTHOR / DATE WRITTEN

Likely Nathan or Gad • c. 1000 BC

MAJOR THEMES — Sovereignty of God,
Desire for a Righteous King

KEY WORDS — Kingship, Covenant, Throne

KEY VERSE

2 SAMUEL 7:16

Your house and kingdom will endure before me forever,
and your throne will be established forever.

2 Samuel 1-3

The beginning of 2 Samuel marks a new beginning for David.

The start of the book introduces us to an Amalekite who tries to take credit for the death of Saul to seemingly win favor with David. But instead of rejoicing like some may have expected over the death of Saul, David mourns. David mourns deeply for the loss of his friend, Jonathan, and the loss of King Saul. It seems that David is well aware of the great tragedy that is playing out before his eyes. David shows us what it means to be a man of sorrow by weeping over the impact of sin on this world, and by doing so, He points us to Jesus.

After the lives of Saul and Jonathan are mourned, the young shepherd boy becomes the king of Judah. We can learn much from David as we notice that he inquires of the Lord before his anointing. He does not assume the Lord's will or act on his own will. He goes to the Lord and seeks direction. David is not anointed as king over the entire nation at first, but first over the small tribe of Judah. Little by little, God is demonstrating His faithfulness to David. Like the kingdom that Jesus will preach of, David's kingdom begins small, but it will grow.

Chapter 3 gives us a sad picture of the impact that sin continues to hold in the land of Israel. The chapter begins with a recounting of David's many wives. David's desire for many wives falls into line with the warnings of 1 Samuel 8 and will ultimately be David's downfall. The rest of the chapter details the story of Abner. Accusations come against him, and though we are never told if they are true, we see his prideful heart throughout the chapter. Over and over, we see people trying to take matters into their own hands. In the end, Abner is murdered by Joab, and sin continues to multiply. David mourned for Abner and ultimately left justice to the Lord.

We are not immune to the desire to take situations into our own hands. Thankfully, this section is a reminder of God's grace for all the times that we do not trust Him and also for the times when we allow sin to creep into our hearts. The hope for our sinful hearts is found in Jesus, who is our better King.

"The hope for our sinful hearts is found in Jesus."

When Saul dies, even though David is free from running and will be king, he still mourns this death. What does this teach us about compassion?

Take a moment to reflect on how David sought the Lord for direction. What are some ways you can more actively seek direction from the Lord?

What do these chapters show you about the impact of sin?

2 Samuel 4-6

We may not always understand God's plan or His ways, but we can always trust in His steadfast love and faithfulness.

In chapter 5, the shepherd boy, David, becomes the shepherd king of the entire nation of Israel. It has been a long and difficult journey to this place, and though David still likely has a heart full of questions, He is confident in the power and presence of God. Sadly, it is soon after his anointing that we see David taking more wives and concubines. Samuel had predicted that kings would take from the people, and Deuteronomy had warned against kings multiplying wives, but David continued down this path (1 Samuel 8, Deuteronomy 17). As we rejoice over the anointing of David, we are also sad over his sin. We realize that though David is a better king than Saul was, and though he is the man who God had appointed to be king, He is not the true and greater King who will come only through Jesus.

The ark that had been carried away is finally returned to Jerusalem, and there is a tragic sequence of events regarding its transportation and the death of Uzzah. God is holy and requires obedience from His people. When the ark is returned, David dances before the Lord in complete joy for all that God has done. Michal, who had faced a difficult life, was disgusted by his undignified behavior. She had good reason to be upset with David for the things that he had done to her, but her bitterness caused her to take that anger out on the good display of worship before the Lord.

God is faithful and good—even when we sin, even in the waiting, even when nothing seems to make sense. He is working His faithful plan in this world, and we can rest in that truth and trust in Jesus, who is our true King.

"God is faithful and good."

Take a moment to reflect on the journey that God had planned for David, from shepherd boy to king of Israel. What does this teach you about God's character?

How does this reinforce to you the idea that God uses weak people to show and prove His strength?

In chapter 6, we read about the intense worship that David gave to the Lord, praising God for all that He had done. How does this encourage you to be more fervent in worshiping the Lord?

2 Samuel 7-9

God keeps His covenant and pursues His people.

Chapter 7 opens with David wanting to build a more permanent house for the Lord. At first, Nathan the prophet thinks it is a great idea, but the Lord reveals to him that David would not be the one to build a house for the Lord, and in this passage, we see some of the most pivotal and beautiful promises of Scripture. The passage is often known as the Davidic covenant, and the language continues to build on the covenant language of the Old Testament. Here the Lord tells David that he will not build a house but that he would have a son who would build a house for the Lord. In the immediate future, David would have Solomon, who would build a beautiful temple. But this is a promise of far more than a physical house. This is a promise of a lineage and a dynasty. This is the promise of one Son who would sit on David's throne forever. This is a promise of Jesus. In the promise to a young girl named Mary in Luke 1:32, we learn that Jesus would sit on the throne of His father, David. And, in us, as the Church, the temple is being built. We are built like living stones into the temple of God through our union with Christ (1 Peter 2:4-8, Ephesians 2:22). David's response is to worship for all God has done, for all He would do, and for all of who He is.

Chapter 8 details more of the victories of David. We are given a picture of a victorious king who governs his people with justice and equity. But David was not perfect. In the coming chapters, we will see this made abundantly clear. But in his strengths and weaknesses, David makes our hearts yearn for the greater King.

In chapter 9, we are shown a picture of the love and mercy we have found in God. David pursues and shows kindness and steadfast love to Jonathan's disabled son. In a culture where new kings would customarily kill the previous king's family, this was radical mercy and grace. David's relationship with Mephibosheth points us to the beauty of who God is and all that He has done for us. We are weak and crippled by sin, and He is the King of all. He calls for us in kindness and mercy. He pursues us and takes us in as we are. He brings us to His table and calls us His own. And because of all God has done for us, we can extend kindness, mercy, and grace to those around us.

"He calls for us in kindness and mercy."

2 Samuel 7:13 reveals a glimpse of Jesus Christ. Reflect on how good God's plans are and how gracious He is to have sent His Son for the atonement of our sins.

In 2 Samuel 8:6, we see that the Lord made David victorious wherever he went. Take a moment to think through why David had success and Saul did not. How does this teach us to pursue God's heart?

David shows Mephibosheth kindness because of the covenant he made with Jonathan. How does this deepen your understanding of the importance of covenants? How does this encourage you to keep your word?

2 Samuel 10-12

In chapter 10, we are given a picture of David as a conquering king who values justice and fights his people.

We see God's faithfulness and are reminded that God always does what He says He will do. But chapter 11 brings us another side of David and leaves us grieving over the imperfection of this chosen king.

At the pinnacle of David's life and career, we see one of his greatest failures. The story of David and Bathsheba is well known and often misunderstood. It all begins when David did not go with his men and stayed home from battle. He was not where he should have been, and it will cost him and all those impacted by this situation dearly. While he was home, he saw a woman bathing on a nearby rooftop. She was cleansing herself from her monthly period, an act of faithfulness to God's law. David is overcome by his lust and inquired about who she was. And though he finds out that she is another man's wife, he sends for her anyway. The text tells us that David took her. Another repetition of what Samuel reminded us in 1 Samuel 8 of what kings would do—they would take. Though often thought of as a picture of adultery or even an affair, this is not the picture that Scripture describes. Bathsheba had no power or rank to resist the king of Israel. We are given no inclination that she desired to go, but David sent for her to be brought to him, and she conceived a child.

The man after God's own heart is pulled away by his lust. Things only worsen as David tries to trick Uriah and eventually has Uriah killed. Chapter 12 shows us how Nathan rebukes David, but his sin still has consequences, and the child of David and Bathsheba dies. It is at this time that David pens the words of Psalm 51. David's sin is great, but His God is greater. Though there are consequences, David finds steadfast love in the Lord. God would eventually give another son who would bring them great joy, and it would be through the line of that son that God would preserve the covenant line of the Messiah. Through David's unfaithfulness, God was still faithful.

Bathsheba was rejected and treated like a mere object. She was sinned against because of David's lust and pride. David was a prideful and sinful man who abused his power and committed murder. And Jesus is the answer for both of them. It is Jesus who was despised and rejected in our place, and He will never reject His own. It is Jesus who bears the sin of His people, bringing forgiveness and restoration. And it is in Jesus that we hope. For our sin and the sin of others against us, our only hope is Jesus.

"Our only hope is Jesus."

Because David did not go out to battle as he should have, he went down a dark and sinful path. How does this illustrate the importance of walking faithfully?

Nathan used an illustration to convey the sin that David had committed. What do we learn from this account?

How is Jesus the answer for our sin and the sin of others against us?

2 Samuel 13-15

Sin brings devastation. It leaves guilt and shame in its wake for those who sinned and those who have been sinned against.

How often we are prone to underestimate the devastating effects of our sin. David certainly did, but he would see the consequences of his sin play out in his family as his sons lived lives that too often mimicked his own. David's son, Amnon, would be so consumed by his lust that he would rape his half-sister, Tamar. Amnon's crafty friend, Joab, is a reminder to us of the crafty serpent of Genesis 3, who looks to the tempted and tells them to take what they see and what they want. Amnon is again a picture for us of "the taking" that Samuel predicted in 1 Samuel 8. Tamar was violated and left desolate by the sin of her brother. And sadly, the reaction of David to the sin of his son and the violation of his daughter was anger that did nothing to bring justice.

David's son, Absalom, was so consumed with his anger and bitterness that he ordered the death of his brother, Amnon. This family of men had become consumed with their sin, selfishness, and lust for women and power. The effects of their sin would devastate their entire family as well as the entire nation. As the passage presses forward, we continue to see Absalom's lust for power. Like Saul before him, Absalom looked like a king but did not have the character of a king. His lust for power would lead him to conspire against his father and steal the affection of the Israelites from the rightful king.

David was fleeing from Jerusalem and was broken-hearted by the sin that had overtaken his family. It is in this state of desperation that David writes the moving words of Psalm 3. The words of this psalm are a powerful reminder that our help comes from the Lord alone.

The weakness of King David and the fallen sons of David points to the true and better son of David, King Jesus. In His perfect life, He did not sin like all of humanity who had gone before. And in His sacrificial death, He paid the price for our sin and shame. He alone is the answer to the weight of sin that crushes guilty souls and the sorrow and suffering of those who have been victims of sin and its curse. As tragic as these stories are, they point us to the only One who has the power to redeem us from the curse of sin.

"He alone is the answer to the weight of sin that crushes guilty souls."

208

QUESTIONS

David's pattern of sin trickled down to his sons. How does this illustrate the importance of our actions around others?

Absalom killed his brother, and David still receives him. How does this exemplify the grace that God shows us?

Take a moment to read Psalm 3. Dwell on these words, and spend time in confident prayer, thanking God for sustaining us.

2 Samuel 16-18

These chapters show the depth and tragedy of
sin and bitterness.

The once seemingly invincible David was under attack from all sides, even
from those who should have been closest to him. He had gone from the
highest of highs to the lowest of lows. David seems to have enemies at every
turn, and at the end of chapter 16, we see that even his own son, Absalom,
is rebelling and revolting against him. In 2 Samuel 12, God had spoken the
consequences of David's sin with Bathsheba, and it is here that we see those
consequences coming to pass. From the same rooftop that David had gazed
lustfully at Bathsheba, Absalom shames his father by violating David's concubines on the rooftop. As so often happens, sin leads to the objectification of
women. The results of sin are devastating and real.

By the time today's passage ends, we see the tragic death of Absalom. We
watch as the son of David hangs on a tree and then is pierced and buried. His
rebellion and sin were paid for with his own life. But this fallen son of David
must shift our gaze to David's true and perfect son who also hanged on a tree
at Calvary, though not for His own sins. He was pierced for our transgres-
sions. He was buried in a tomb of stone. But the true son of David was not
held by the grave, for He rose victorious over our sin and death.

David wept when he heard the news of the death of Absalom. He grieved,
and he mourned. But through it all, God was faithful, and He never left
David's side. Yet even a tragic story like this points us to Jesus. It points us
to the answer to David's tragic story and the answer for our own sin and rebellion. We do not need to live in our sin because Jesus has gone to the cross
for us. And though hope may have seemed lost for a moment, the promises
of David's everlasting kingdom were not on a son named Absalom but on
a son named Jesus. God would keep His promises to David and us. His
faithfulness is not dependent on us but on His gracious character. He will
do what He has said He will do.

"His faithfulness is not dependent on us but
on His gracious character."

In chapter 16, we see that Ziba stays with David because of the kindness he showed to Mephibosheth. How does this reinforce that the care we show other people truly matters?

In chapter 17, we see that David is again waiting to return to the kingdom God had given him. How does his example of patience encourage you?

This section ends with David weeping over Absolom's death, yet God never leaves David's side. How does this speak to the reality that though we feel pain, God is still near to us?

2 Samuel 19-21

Though Absalom had betrayed him, and the nation had paid the price, David still grieves the loss of his son. After Joab's rebuke and prompting of David, he returned to Jerusalem, and the hearts of the men of Judah were softened toward him. Though the people had rebelled and followed Absalom, they quickly return to David, who they know is God's anointed king for Israel. We then see David extend grace and mercy to those around him. Despite the deception of Ziba, Mephibosheth is welcomed back into David's home as his faithful, adopted son (2 Samuel 9:1-13). Mephibosheth had mourned for David and been faithful to David throughout the journey. As we remember how David is a picture for us of Jesus and Mephibosheth is a picture of weak and wounded sinners who have been rescued by grace, we can now see how Mephibosheth is an example of faithfulness to us as well.

Amid the cruelty of Joab and as the nation picks up the pieces from the tragedy it has endured, a familiar nation comes again. The Israelites vowed never to destroy the Gibeonites back in Joshua 9, but Saul, who had been aware of this vow, had disregarded it. The author of 1 and 2 Samuel consistently shows us the differences between David and Saul, and this is no exception. Though Saul was a covenant breaker, David is a covenant keeper. He keeps the covenant with the Gibeonites, and he also keeps his covenant with Jonathan by sparing Mephibosheth. It is a sad day when the sons of Saul are given to the Gibeonites, but it serves as a reminder that God takes our vows seriously. The ending of David's life is much like the beginning. David's story, in many ways, began with the killing of Goliath, and now we see the warrior king sending his men to fight another giant and continue to have victory over the Philistines as God had promised.

These stories are full of tragedy and heartbreak. We see in them the consequences of sin. But we also see the faithfulness of God, who does not leave His people, who showers us in grace, and who extends mercy to the weak and the vulnerable. As we rejoice over the restoration of King David, our hearts also long for King Jesus.

"As we rejoice over the restoration of King David, our hearts also long for King Jesus."

In chapter 19, we see David show grace to a variety of people. How does this reflect the way that God treats His children? And how does it inform how we should treat others?

God cares about the covenant that was made with the Gibeonites. How does this deepen your understanding of what a covenant is?

In chapter 21, we see that David finally gave a proper burial to Saul and Jonathan as a final tribute to the covenant he had made with Jonathan. How does this spur you on to finish what you start and remain true to your word?

2 Samuel 22-24

David was not a perfect man, and we have seen sin and its consequences over and over throughout his life. This psalm, written at the end of his life, is a shining testament to God's covenantal love to David. David was not always faithful, but God was always faithful and true. David's song of deliverance recorded in 2 Samuel 22 reminds us to run to the Lord in praise for all that He has done and for all of who He is. Throughout his entire life, David consistently ran back to the Lord in repentance and for help. We see here that David was thoroughly convinced of God's goodness no matter what circumstances life brought. 2 Samuel 22 and the corresponding Psalm 18 remind us that God is holy and majestic while also being merciful and personal. The Lord is our rock, fortress, deliverer, God, refuge, shield, salvation, stronghold, Savior, rescuer, support, rewarder, light, and so much more. When David reflected on the present and past, He knew God was with him and had been with him every step of the way. David's beautiful song ends with a reminder of God's steadfast love and the promise of the Davidic covenant. Just as God had been faithful to David, God would be faithful to establish the Davidic king, Jesus, who reigns forever and ever.

The final chapter of David's story finds David at the end of his life, choosing to take a census and disobeying the Lord. It seems that David was finding his security and pride in an army instead of in the Lord, and he immediately repented, knowing that he had sinned against the Lord. Though there were consequences to pay for his sin, God was present and showed His faithfulness. David bought a piece of land to sacrifice to the Lord after his sin, and one day that same piece of land would be the place where the temple is built by Solomon (2 Chronicles 3:1). It is a sweet reminder that even in David's sin, God had not forgotten him. God would be faithful to His covenant with David.

The story of David is filled with triumph and tragedy. We love David, but we are also so often disappointed by him. But his story is meant to do this. It is meant to leave us longing for the son of David. The son of David is the fulfillment of God's covenant with David, and we rejoice as the people of God grafted into that covenant.

"God was always faithful and true."

214

QUESTIONS

How does the song in chapter 22, along with the corresponding Psalm 18, deepen your worship of God?

How does David's story leave us longing for Jesus, the son of David?

Now that you have completed reading Genesis through 2 Samuel, take time to reflect on what you have learned about God and His character. Spend some time in prayer, praising God for His faithfulness, His holiness, and His continual provision.

WHAT IS THE GOSPEL?

THANK YOU FOR READING AND ENJOYING THIS STUDY WITH US!
WE ARE ABUNDANTLY GRATEFUL FOR THE WORD OF GOD, THE INSTRUCTION
WE GLEAN FROM IT, AND THE EVER-GROWING UNDERSTANDING IT PROVIDES
FOR US OF GOD'S CHARACTER. WE ARE ALSO THANKFUL THAT SCRIPTURE
CONTINUALLY POINTS TO ONE THING IN INNUMERABLE WAYS: THE GOSPEL.

We remember our brokenness when we read about the fall of Adam and Eve in the garden of Eden (Genesis 3), when sin entered into a perfect world and maimed it. We remember the necessity that something innocent must die to pay for our sin when we read about the atoning sacrifices in the Old Testament. We read that we have all sinned and fallen short of the glory of God (Romans 3:23) and that the penalty for our brokenness, the wages of our sin, is death (Romans 6:23). We all are in need of grace and mercy, but most importantly, we all need a Savior.

We consider the goodness of God when we realize that He did not plan to leave us in this dire state. We see His promise to buy us back from the clutches of sin and death in Genesis 3:15. And we see that promise accomplished with Jesus Christ on the cross. Jesus Christ knew no sin yet became sin so that we might become righteous through His sacrifice (2 Corinthians 5:21). Jesus was tempted in every way that we are and lived sinlessly. He was reviled yet still yielded Himself for our sake, that we may have life abundant in Him. Jesus lived the perfect life that we could not live and died the death that we deserved.

The gospel is profound yet simple. There are many mysteries in it that we can never exhaust this side of heaven, but there is still overwhelming weight to its implications in this life. The gospel is the telling of our sinfulness and God's goodness, and this gracious gift compels a response. We are saved by grace through faith, which means

that we rest with faith in the grace that Jesus Christ displayed on the cross (Ephesians 2:8-9). We cannot save ourselves from our brokenness or do any amount of good works to merit God's favor, but we can have faith that what Jesus accomplished in His death, burial, and resurrection was more than enough for our salvation and our eternal delight. When we accept God, we are commanded to die to our self and our sinful desires and live a life worthy of the calling we have received (Ephesians 4:1). The gospel compels us to be sanctified, and in so doing, we are conformed to the likeness of Christ Himself. This is hope. This is redemption. This is the gospel.

SCRIPTURE TO REFERENCE:

GENESIS 3:15
I will put hostility between you and the woman, and between your offspring and her offspring. He will strike your head, and you will strike his heel.

ROMANS 3:23
For all have sinned and fall short of the glory of God.

ROMANS 6:23
For the wages of sin is death, but the gift of God is eternal life in Christ Jesus our Lord.

2 CORINTHIANS 5:21
He made the one who did not know sin to be sin for us, so that in him we might become the righteousness of God.

EPHESIANS 2:8-9
For you are saved by grace through faith, and this is not from yourselves; it is God's gift — not from works, so that no one can boast.

EPHESIANS 4:1
Therefore I, the prisoner in the Lord, urge you to walk worthy of the calling you have received,

*Thank you for studying
God's Word with us!*

CONNECT WITH US

@thedailygraceco
@kristinschmucker

CONTACT US

info@thedailygraceco.com

SHARE

#thedailygraceco
#lampandlight

VISIT US ONLINE

www.thedailygraceco.com

MORE DAILY GRACE

The Daily Grace App
Daily Grace Podcast